Praise for *Practice for Heaven*

One of his classmates from seven decades ago in Rome once told me, "Even back then, when Eddie Egan spoke, we listened; when he wrote, we read." As Cardinal Egan's grateful successor, I heartily agree. Thanks to this welcome work of Dr. McAleer, we can now all enjoy the wonderfully effective prose of this master teacher.

— Timothy Michael Cardinal Dolan
Archbishop of New York

Life with its varied problems, some tragic, some gently humorous, passes before our eyes in a series of observant little stories or portraits. Short they may be, but their content (since it concerns humanity) is serious, with a message for each of us. This is a book of hope for every age, for men and women, old or young; for folk believing in God, and for those who don't. The book's inevitable Catholic slant is never offensive or judgmental but always compassionate. A great reader himself, the cardinal will live on in these articles to influence and comfort whoever reads them.

— Virginia Barton
Oxford, England

Practice for Heaven

Practice for Heaven

True Stories from a Modern Missionary

by Edward Cardinal Egan

Edited by Dr. Joseph McAleer

SOPHIA INSTITUTE PRESS
Manchester, New Hampshire

Sophia Institute Press
Box 5284, Manchester, NH 03108
1-800-888-9344

www.SophiaInstitute.com

Sophia Institute Press® is a registered trademark of Sophia Institute.

Library of Congress Cataloging-in-Publication Data

Names: Egan, Edward M., 1932-2015, author. | McAleer, Joseph, editor.
Title: Practice for heaven : true stories from a modern missionary / Edward Cardinal Egan ; edited by Dr. Joseph McAleer.
Description: Manchester, New Hampshire : Sophia Institute Press, 2016.
Identifiers: LCCN 2016004361 | ISBN 9781622823413 (pbk. : alk. paper)
Subjects: LCSH: Egan, Edward M., 1932-2015. | Cardinals — New York — Biography. | Catholic Church — United States — Clergy — Biography.
Classification: LCC BX4705.E325 A3 2016 | DDC 282.092 — dc23 LC record available at http://lccn.loc.gov/2016004361

First printing

Contents

∽

Starting Young

∽

A Priest's Life

≈

Beyond the Sea

≈

Enlightenment

⤺

Holy Men and Women

⤺

Respecting Life

Acknowledgments

This book could not have been completed in accordance with the late Cardinal Egan's wishes without the assistance and co-operation of a number of individuals.

In the Archdiocese of New York, special appreciation is extended to Cardinal Egan's successor, Timothy Cardinal Dolan; and to Monsignor Gregory Mustaciuolo, Vicar General and Chancellor, for obtaining the approval and blessing of the cardinal's estate for the publication of his writings. James P. Mc-Cabe, Esq., General Counsel for the Archdiocese, facilitated this process.

At the Chapel of the Sacred Hearts of Jesus and Mary in New York City, where Cardinal Egan resided, Father Douglas Crawford, the cardinal's secretary, and Margaret Rice offered hospitality and support. Catherine Triglia Murphy was an expert typist.

In the Diocese of Bridgeport, brother priests and former colleagues of Cardinal Egan offered insight and advice, including Monsignor Stephen M. DiGiovanni, H.E.D., Monsignor Thomas W. Powers, Father Michael K. Jones, Dr. Joan M. Kelly, Brian D. Wallace, and John R. Glover. Father James K. McConica, C.S.B., Rosemary Giedroyé, and Kasia Parham lent an international perspective.

Finally, a debt of gratitude is owed to the hard-working editors and staffs of *Fairfield County Catholic* and *Catholic New York*, in whose publications these "Articles of Faith" first appeared.

—Dr. Joseph McAleer, Editor

Introduction

Ask anyone who knew His Eminence, Edward Cardinal Egan, and they will inevitably remember two things: his distinctive baritone ("The voice of God," one Catholic school first-grader described it) and his diocesan newspaper column. The latter was a labor of love for the cardinal, who took the task seriously, revising multiple drafts before publication. Over twenty-one years as an ordinary of dioceses in Connecticut and New York, he wrote more than 230 newspaper columns, either for *Fairfield County Catholic* or *Catholic New York*.

The cardinal connected with readers through a writing style akin to storytelling, precise and elegant, yet approachable. His mission was the same as that of any Roman Catholic priest: to teach the Faith. Whether recounting a past experience in a parish or in Rome, or carefully delivering a catechetical lesson, the cardinal drew you in as a trusted listener and a faith-filled friend. He was also not afraid to proclaim boldly on controversial issues of the day, including abortion.

In simplest terms, the cardinal was an evangelizer, a modern missionary. All of his efforts as a priest were "practice" for getting into Heaven, as explained in one of what he called his "Articles of Faith."

Practice for Heaven

For years, admirers of his writings appealed to the cardinal to publish a book. In retirement, he acquiesced. At the time of his death in March 2015, he had culled fifty columns. He thoroughly enjoyed the vetting process but (predictably) revised each article multiple times, displaying his usual insistence on correct punctuation and grammar. They are now published here with the permission of the cardinal's estate.

The cardinal's columns are arranged thematically in six categories but can be enjoyed at random, too. This is a commonplace-like book to be shared and savored, to pick up and put down, enjoyed at leisure in one sitting or several. The stories within—all true (some names have been changed)—contain grace-filled moments that always instruct, frequently entertain, and sometimes astonish. They represent well a master storyteller at his best.

≈

Edward Michael Egan was born on April 2, 1932, in Oak Park, Illinois, the third of four children to Thomas and Genevieve (Costello) Egan. His father managed sales in the Chicago area for the Emerson Electric Manufacturing Company.

The Egans belonged to Saint Giles Parish, and the children attended the parish elementary school, staffed by the Dominican Sisters of Sinsinawa, Wisconsin. "The parish was our life," Cardinal Egan recalled. "It was our center. It was the source of our friends. What a gift to be reared in that kind of an environment."

At the age of eight, Edward and his older brother, Thomas, contracted poliomyelitis and were homebound for the better part of two years. "I couldn't walk or move, with an aspirator by my side," the cardinal recalled. "I remember my mom and dad saying, 'Oh Eddie, we'll get you out of this.' They were fighters, in a quiet way. That was the old way that people handled things." Edward and Thomas escaped the long-term ravages of polio thanks to the "Sister Kenny System" suggested by a doctor from the March of Dimes. The experience would instill in the young Edward a drive to succeed at anything he undertook in the future, particularly academics.

Sensing a call to ministry, a parish priest enrolled Edward in Quigley Preparatory Seminary in Chicago, which nurtured his love of learning and music, especially the piano. He was editor of the school newspaper and yearbook and president of the graduating class.

At that time, only 15 percent of Quigley graduates went on to seminary. "When I was about seventeen, I said to myself, 'Now, Eddie, I think it's time you asked: Where do you stand on all this?'" the cardinal remembered. "Certainly a career in music wasn't for me. I knew priesthood was it. I had made my decision." His parents were supportive. "'Whatever you kids want to do, do it well' was their attitude," the cardinal said. "My Grandmother Egan said, 'Eddie, if you're going to become a priest, go all the way and become a Jesuit.' That was the attitude at the time."

Edward did not choose the Society of Jesus. Instead, he went on to earn a bachelor's degree in philosophy from Saint Mary of the Lake Seminary in Mundelein, Illinois. The cardinal credited his seminary rector, Monsignor Malachy Foley, with a valuable lesson on the priesthood. In 1951, Monsignor Foley invited the nineteen-year-old seminarian into his office and informed him that he would be going to Rome for major seminary.

"In the course of our conversation, he delivered one of the best sermons I have ever heard," the cardinal recalled. "It climaxed as follows: 'Eddie, come back from Rome a holy priest who never seeks an assignment and never turns one down, and

I can assure you a life of deep-down priestly happiness.' I have had many occasions to reflect on his words over the years that followed that meeting."

Completing his seminary studies at the Pontifical North American College in Vatican City, Edward was ordained on December 15, 1957, by the rector, Bishop Martin J. O'Connor. In 1958, Father Egan received a Licentiate in Sacred Theology from the Pontifical Gregorian University.

After ordination, Father Egan returned to the United States, where he served as one of nine curates at Holy Name Cathedral Parish in Chicago. His duties included teaching "inquiry classes" for prospective Catholics and making chaplain rounds at a nearby hospital.

"To say that I was happy in my assignment would be a colossal understatement," the cardinal recalled. "It was everything that I had hoped for in seminary, and more." But within two months, Father Egan was reassigned as the new assistant chancellor of the Archdiocese of Chicago and secretary to Albert Cardinal Meyer, the first of a series of prominent appointments.

In 1960, Father Egan returned to Rome as assistant vice-rector and "repetitor" (a tutor who gave classes) of moral theology and canon law at the Pontifical North American College. In 1964, he earned a doctorate in canon law summa cum laude from the Pontifical Gregorian University. He then returned to Chicago, where he served as secretary to John Cardinal Cody.

Cardinal Cody asked now-Monsignor Egan to establish two new commissions for the archdiocese: one on ecumenism and interfaith relations, and the other on social justice, primarily to do with racial equality in employment and housing. In this capacity Monsignor Egan worked with Dr. Martin Luther King Jr. to arrange peaceful marches for "open housing" in various neighborhoods of the city in 1968, only weeks before Dr. King was assassinated.

"A few weeks later, I found myself in a police car with Cardinal Cody and Mayor Richard Daley, driving into the Westside of Chicago filled with rioters and bright with orange flames against the evening sky," the cardinal recalled. "The rioting ended with an agreement between Dr. King's followers and the political, business, and religious leadership of Chicago that created the Leadership Council for Metropolitan Open Communities, of which I was a vice chair."

In 1969, Monsignor Egan was named co-chancellor of the Archdiocese of Chicago and continued the work begun on ecumenism and social justice. For nearly a year he also served as pastor of Saint Leo's, an African-American parish with a Catholic school. He would recall this time as among the happiest of his priesthood.

～

In 1971, Monsignor Egan returned to Rome as a judge of the Tribunal of the Sacred Roman Rota, a position he held until his episcopal consecration in 1985. In this capacity he was one of the "guards" of the conclaves that elected Pope John Paul I and Pope John Paul II in 1978.

While in Rome, Monsignor Egan was also a professor of canon law at the Pontifical Gregorian University; a professor of civil and criminal procedure at the Studium Rotale, the law school of the Rota; a commissioner of the Congregation for the Sacraments and Divine Worship; and a consultor of the Congregation for the Clergy.

Monsignor Egan was one of six canonists who reviewed the new *Code of Canon Law* with Pope John Paul II before its promulgation in 1983. "The regular meetings that we were privileged to have with the Holy Father were an altogether unforgettable blessing," the cardinal remembered.

Monsignor Egan was consecrated a bishop on May 22, 1985, in the Basilica of Saints John and Paul in Rome by Bernardin Cardinal Gantin, prefect of the Sacred Congregation for Bishops. John Cardinal O'Connor, Archbishop of New York, and Bishop John R. Keating of Arlington, Virginia, were co-consecrators.

From 1985 to 1988 Bishop Egan served as auxiliary bishop and vicar for education of the Archdiocese of New York. The latter put him in charge of Catholic schools; the catechetical program for children and adults; campus ministry; vocations; and the pro-life and family-life offices.

"My years as an auxiliary bishop taught me many lessons that proved to be invaluable when I became the ordinary of a diocese, and later of an archdiocese," the cardinal observed. "The most important might be summed up as follows: When dealing with a controversial issue, keep calm, avoid grandstanding, and say only what absolutely needs to be said. Sound and fury may beget notoriety for some, but regularly result in failure for the cause they champion."

⁓

On November 8, 1988, Pope John Paul II appointed Bishop Egan to be the third bishop of the Diocese of Bridgeport in Fairfield County, Connecticut. He was installed on December 14, 1988.

Bishop Egan oversaw the regionalization of diocesan elementary schools; established Hispanic and Haitian apostolates;

founded the Saint John Fisher Seminary Residence for young men considering the priesthood; reorganized diocesan health-care facilities; and initiated the Inner-City Foundation for Charity and Education. He saw to the construction of the Catherine Dennis Keefe Queen of the Clergy Residence for Retired Priests and the establishment of the Saint Catherine Academy for Children with Special Needs and the Haitian Catholic Center.

The sexual abuse of children by priests was an issue confronted by Bishop Egan during his tenure in Bridgeport as well as in New York. "There can be no doubt: sexual abuse of children is an abomination," the cardinal declared in 2002. "It is both immoral and illegal, and I will not tolerate it. Be assured that I will continue to do everything in my power to ensure the safety and security of every child. Should any priest sexually abuse a child, he will be removed from pastoral ministry. My heart goes out to any and all victims and their families."

All of the cases that Bishop Egan faced in Bridgeport concerned priestly misconduct that had occurred prior to his arrival in 1988. Nonetheless, he took swift action according to the prevailing wisdom of the time.

"The procedure we followed was to send the accused to the most celebrated (and expensive) psychiatric institution in the Northeast, abide by the directives of its psychiatrists in every detail, and pray," the cardinal recalled. "It was, however, quite futile. I lost all confidence in the analyses and forecasts of even the most highly esteemed exponents of the psychiatric community. The course of action that we were following had, however, somehow become approved by even our bitterest critics; and frankly, we knew nowhere else to turn." Litigation ensued, and the Bridgeport cases were eventually settled out of court.

Practice for Heaven

⁓

On May 11, 2000, Pope John Paul II appointed Bishop Egan as the ninth archbishop of New York. He was installed at Saint Patrick's Cathedral on June 19, 2000, by Archbishop Gabriel Montalvo, apostolic nuncio to the United States.

Pope John Paul II elevated Archbishop Egan to the College of Cardinals in the Consistory of February 21, 2001. He was assigned as his titular church the Basilica of Saints John and Paul on the Caelian Hill in Rome.

In July 2001, Cardinal Egan was named by Pope John Paul II to serve in September and October of that year as the moderator of a synod of Bishops in Rome. His assistant was Jorge Cardinal Bergoglio, archbishop of Buenos Aires. When Cardinal Bergoglio was elected to the See of Peter in 2013, his friend was overjoyed. "Twelve years earlier I had come to know the humble, generous archbishop of Buenos Aires and admire him immensely," the cardinal said.

On September 11, 2001, and on many days to follow, Cardinal Egan was at Ground Zero to anoint and absolve the dead and injured from the terrorist attack on the World Trade Center. "The horror that engulfed us defied description," the cardinal remembered. "Smoke and ash were coming from above and below. I opened black plastic body bags so as to absolve and anoint the individuals inside. I knelt, often in water, to absolve and anoint others, both conscious and unconscious, who had been struck by falling beams and debris or who were overcome by the thick, stifling air."

⁓

During Cardinal Egan's tenure as archbishop of New York, the number of registered parishioners increased; the budget of

Catholic Charities more than doubled; enrollment in Catholic elementary and secondary schools grew; the archdiocesan news-paper, *Catholic New York*, became the largest in the nation; and the archdiocese and its various agencies were made debt free. In 2001, Cardinal Egan opened a new facility for the Saint John Neumann Seminary and Hall in Yonkers, New York.

In 2004, he established the John Cardinal O'Connor Residence for retired priests of the archdiocese in the Riverdale area of the Bronx. In 2006, he inaugurated the "Catholic Channel" on Sirius/XM Satellite Radio, providing Catholic programming twenty-four hours a day, seven days a week, throughout the United States and Canada. In 2008, he authorized and funded the construction of a new campus ministry center at New York University in Manhattan.

On April 19, 2006, Cardinal Egan participated in the conclave that elected Pope Benedict XVI. In 2008, on the occasion of the two hundredth anniversary of the founding of the diocese (later, archdiocese) of New York, Cardinal Egan had the honor of welcoming Pope Benedict XVI to New York for a pastoral visit that included the celebration of Mass by the Holy Father in Saint Patrick's Cathedral and in Yankee Stadium.

As in Bridgeport, Cardinal Egan was proactive in dealing with the priest abuse crisis in New York. Soon after his arrival in 2000, he engaged a law firm to go through the files of every priest of the archdiocese dating back fifty years to identify any cases that might need attention.

"The undertaking lasted almost a year and was very costly," the cardinal recalled. "Nevertheless, when it was completed, each district attorney in the three boroughs and five counties served by the archdiocese was given all the relevant files for his or her area, and within my second year all files were closed officially."

During his tenure as archbishop of New York, he added, "There was no known case of the sexual abuse of a minor by a priest of the archdiocese, though there was one accusation which was tried judicially at the direction of the Holy See and concluded with a verdict of innocence for the priest in question."

Over one weekend in 2002, in a letter read during every Sunday Mass in the archdiocese of New York, Cardinal Egan offered an apology.

> Over the past fifteen years, in both Bridgeport and New York, I consistently sought and acted upon the best independent advice available to me from medical experts and behavioral scientists. It is clear that today we have a much better understanding of this problem. If in hindsight we also discover that mistakes may have been made as regards prompt removal of priests and assistance to victims, I am deeply sorry.

On February 23, 2009, at the age of seventy-seven, Cardinal Egan was retired as archbishop of New York. He continued to reside in Manhattan and assist in the works of the archdiocese, while serving on a number of offices of the Vatican, until his death on March 5, 2015, one month short of his eighty-third birthday.

On March 9, 2015, in Saint Patrick's Cathedral, Bishop Dennis Sullivan of Camden, New Jersey, delivered the homily at the vigil Mass for Cardinal Egan. He captured the spirit of a towering cleric who was, at heart, a humble parish priest and a born preacher.

> Jesus preached in the Nazareth synagogue. I could not say if the Lord preached with the meticulous preparation of Edward Egan—agonizing over every word he spoke, focused on the details of the Sacred Word in order to transmit God's Word to God's people. "May I tell you a story?..."
>
> Like an Irish storyteller, a *shanachie*, he wove the stories into well-crafted preaching. Never was this pulpit used to condemn anyone. Preaching was to lift up, not to put down; to encourage, not to criticize; to lead all to the mercy and infinite understanding of God...
>
> In the Windy City, in the Eternal City, in the City on the Sound, and in the City That Never Sleeps—in each of them Edward Egan did what a good parish priest does: he rolled up his sleeves and worked at priestly ministry, by which he led his people to God. To our God whom he knew by faith, and now by sight. To our God in whose peace he now rests from his labors, awaiting the Day of Resurrection.

The following day, Timothy Cardinal Dolan delivered the homily at the Mass of Christian Burial for his predecessor as archbishop of New York. "When Pope Saint John Paul II would remark, as he often did, that, 'Love for Jesus and His Church must be the passion of your lives,' no one would smile more broadly, nod more vigorously, and applaud more exuberantly than Edward Egan," Cardinal Dolan said.

> Visiting the priests' lot at one of our cemeteries, he once pointed out to me the inscription on one tombstone:

Dilexit ecclesiam. He liked it, not just because it was in Latin, but because of what it said: "He loved the Church!"

"What a tribute," he commented to me.

A tribute, my friends, Edward Egan also merits, because *dilexit ecclesiam*—he loved the Church. And so I call him a churchman, a term that cannot be reduced to describing a man who prefers brick-and-mortar, ledgers, and an aloof institution, but a man who sees in the Church Jesus Christ, His Lord and Savior, alive in teaching, serving, and sanctifying.

⁌

A master of telling anecdotes, Cardinal Egan will have the last word.

Some months before Pope Benedict XVI retired, Cardinal Dolan and I were in Rome for a Synod, at the conclusion of which we spoke briefly with the Holy Father. In the course of his remarks, Cardinal Dolan told the pontiff, "Cardinal Egan is my best 'Auxiliary Bishop.'"

Somewhat taken aback, Pope Benedict turned toward me for confirmation of Cardinal Dolan's statement. I gave it willingly, adding that I hoped to be of assistance however I can and as long as I can.

The Holy Father continued to seem perplexed. All the same, he whispered, "Bravo, bravo, *Eminenza.*"

Practice for Heaven

Starting Young

From that day forward an impressive number of Stella Maris campers were to be found in the little frame chapel at seven in the morning. Some fidgeted a good deal. Others appeared to be praying with a fervor that belied their years. All, however, described what they were doing in the same way. They were practicing with Father Cas for Heaven.

Heaven Practice

The Stella Maris Summer Camp for Boys boasted an impressive collection of white framed buildings, all well constructed and well maintained, on the shores of Lake Michigan, a few miles east of a tiny Wisconsin town by the name of Oostburg.

In the summer of 1947, I was one of the six camp counselors, all from the minor seminary of the Archdiocese of Chicago, who were supervising the activities of seventy-five campers who ranged in age from nine to thirteen. The camp was owned by a Chicago priest who taught Latin at the minor seminary. He was a tall, portly man of Polish heritage whom everyone called Father Cas.

Each morning Father Cas offered Mass at seven o'clock with his two sisters, their husbands, and three or four of the camp staff in attendance. The liturgy was celebrated with great devotion in a small but handsomely decorated chapel that was the centerpiece of the compound.

⁓

Early in the first week of the season, the campers were in the dining room one morning, having breakfast and making the usual boys-camp noise. Returning from his prayers after Mass,

Father Cas, who ate in a separate dining room with his relatives, looked in on us.

"Counselors, there is much too much racket in here," he announced. "And you boys," he added, "eat your breakfasts, and do your shouting afterward."

The dining room was engulfed in an eerie silence. Father Cas allowed the quiet to make its impression and turned to leave. Suddenly, one of the boys at my table, a twin about ten years of age, called out, "Father Cas, why do you say Mass here every day? Where we live, people go to Mass on Sunday."

The priest reentered the dining room and, veteran teacher that he was, put on his face the look of someone pondering a weighty philosophical question. He paused, seemed about to speak, paused again, and then, confident that he had won the attention of all, launched into a reply.

"Mass," he said, "is practice for Heaven. I am going to Heaven someday, and I want to be good at doing what they do there." He surveyed the dining room, assured himself that all eyes were still on him, and continued. "You see, in Heaven, we will spend morning, noon, and night in the presence of God Himself. We will see Him in all of His wonder and glory. We will love Him, and He will love us in return. And seeing and loving Him, and being seen and loved by Him, will make us so happy that there is no way we could be happier."

His eyes flashed, and for a moment he pretended to be seeing something up in the air toward the ceiling. Quickly, he dropped his glance and changed his tone and mien.

"Each morning," he confined in a stage whisper, "I am in the presence of my God at Holy Mass, not in exactly the same way as I will be in Heaven, but in a marvelous and thrilling way all the same. Jesus Christ, the Second Person of the Most Holy

Trinity, is on the altar under the appearances of bread and wine; and I receive Him — Body, Blood, Soul, and Divinity — into my own heart and soul, where I love Him with all my heart and He loves me with all His heart. That's as close to Heaven as anyone gets here on earth."

He paused again as if to contemplate the power and truth of what he had said and resumed his theme. "Mass is practice for Heaven," he proclaimed. "So I have Mass not just on Sunday, but every day. And nothing in this world could possibly mean more to me."

With that, Father Cas left the dining room. No one dared to speak lest the spell he had woven be broken. The only sounds to be heard were the clink-clink of the glasses and silverware. We all knew what baseball practice was. We all knew what basketball practice was. Many of us even knew what choir practice was. Now we knew more clearly, more compellingly than ever what Mass was. It was Heaven practice.

From that day forward an impressive number of Stella Maris campers were to be found in the little frame chapel at seven in the morning. Some fidgeted a good deal. Others appeared to be praying with a fervor that belied their years. All, however, described what they were doing in the same way. They were practicing with Father Cas for Heaven.

〜

In April of 1969, Father Cas went to his Lord. Several weeks after the funeral, I was standing in line to buy tokens at the North Avenue subway station in Chicago. A man in his early thirties approached me somewhat diffidently.

"Are you Father Egan?" he asked.

"Yes, I am," I replied.

"Do you remember me?" he went on. I confessed that I did not.

"I will give you a clue," he continued. "My wife, two sons, and I were just over at Holy Name Cathedral for ..." he hesitated with a playful twinkle in his eye, "for Heaven practice."

My mind raced back thirty-some years. This was the twin who had asked Father Cas why we had Mass every day at the Stella Maris Camp.

"Of course I remember you now!" I exclaimed. "How have you been, and how is your brother?"

"I've been fine, and my brother is fine too," he answered. "My brother is married and has two daughters. And you know, Father, in both of our families we never say we are going to Mass. We always say we are going to Heaven practice."

His wife and sons beamed over the sharing of a treasured family tradition, and I beamed too.

The next morning the eternal rest of the soul of Father Cas was the intention of my Mass; that is to say, of my practicing for Heaven.

Bridgeport, August 1990

Repairs and Resolutions

New Year's is the traditional time for resolutions. Some are made lightly and quickly forgotten, while others are well thought through and often do more good than is commonly believed. Like most priests, I am regularly asked after Christmas to offer suggestions for New Year's resolutions, and my response is always the same.

When possible, I like to tell two little stories to explain the response and perhaps make it a bit more compelling. Here are the stories.

~

In the fourth-grade classroom of my parish school some sixty-seven years ago, there was a rather elaborate Christmas crèche that stood in a corner on a large cotton-covered table and boasted an impressive stable with a straw roof and a colorful set of plaster statues, some of which stood a foot high.

One day, shortly before Christmas, a tall, ungainly boy rushed past the crèche and knocked one of the plaster shepherds to the ground. The boy apologized profusely, and the Sister who taught the class calmed him immediately. It was an accident, she observed, and accidents will happen.

The next day, another boy came to class to share with all of us what he termed "great news." In a toy store where he was in the habit of purchasing components for model planes, there were also crèches on sale, he reported. One of them, he noted, matched the crèche in our classroom perfectly. Moreover, the enterprising boy had learned from one of the store clerks that individual statues from the crèche were available to be bought for a price that the youngster characterized as "not too bad." Thus, he proposed that we take up a collection and buy a new shepherd.

All agreed enthusiastically — except Sister. She had taken the broken shepherd to the school janitor, she announced, and he had glued the shoulder and arm back onto the statue. The glue was drying and, in due course, Sister assured us, the shepherd would reclaim his place in the crèche.

"It's actually a blessing," Sister observed, "that we have a broken and repaired shepherd in our crèche. For it reminds us at Christmastime that we are all, in a sense, broken. We don't always tell the truth. We often daydream at Mass when we should be speaking to the Lord. We may even take things that aren't ours.

"And about this," she added, "we should not be at all surprised. In one of his epistles, Saint John, the Beloved Disciple of the Lord, wrote that if we say we have never sinned, we are liars. No one is perfect. In all lives there is a certain amount of breakage, as much as we wish there were not.

"But we can be repaired," Sister proclaimed with considerable emotion in her ordinarily restrained voice, "and we all know how. The Lord, who forgave Saint Peter, Saint Thomas, and many others, arranged that we be forgiven in a way that leaves no doubt about the forgiveness as long as we are truly sorry for what we have done. This is, of course, Confession, the sacrament of Penance. That's where we get forgiven. That's where we get repaired. That's where we restore our friendship with the Son of God, Who came on earth at Christmastime to save us from our sins. Our shepherd was broken, but he is being repaired. Soon he will be back in the crèche close to the newborn King.

"The same is true of us," Sister continued. "When we sin, we need to get ourselves repaired as soon as possible. No waiting. No hesitation. No embarrassment. You just go to Confession and put yourself back in the embrace of the Lord, Who loves you and yearns to forgive you — and me, too — whenever we need it."

The next day, the shepherd was restored to his corner of the crèche. We inspected him carefully to see where the shoulder and arm had been attached. No one could be sure. The janitor had done a splendid job.

⌒

More than thirty years later, I was in charge of a parish in a troubled inner-city neighborhood on the South Side of Chicago. At Christmastime, a committee of men and women set up the parish crèche with remarkable speed and care. Poinsettias were put in place, straw was added to the stable floor, the angel's wing was straightened out, and I was invited to come to see the final product. I congratulated the committee most enthusiastically but wondered where the Magi were.

"Do you wait until Epiphany to put them out?" I inquired.

"No," the chair of the parish council replied. "Two of the Magi were badly damaged three years ago. Their heads were broken off when we were repacking the crèche. We don't use them anymore."

"Could we have them repaired?" I asked.

"We tried," a committee member responded. "But the glue would never hold. The heads are too heavy. The only thing that works is duct tape, and that looks terrible."

I told them about the broken shepherd of my childhood and wondered if they would reconsider the duct-tape approach. There was little enthusiasm for the suggestion. Nonetheless, on New Year's Day, as I made my way to the altar for the parish Mass at noon, I noticed that there were in the crèche three Magi, two of them with heads attached with duct tape and, frankly, not looking at all bad, at least to me.

After the Gospel, I put into my pocket the notes I had prepared for the homily and went over to the crèche to speak from there. Once again, I told the story of the broken shepherd in my parish school and all of a sudden found myself repeating the lesson about brokenness and sinfulness that I had heard many years before from a wise and devout religious woman.

"Like the Magi here in our crèche," I said, "we are all in a sense broken. For we are all sinners — some more, others less — but all without exception. We therefore need to be repaired. We need to have our sins wiped away by an all-loving God, Who wishes nothing so much as to forgive our faults and failings and keep us ever in His embrace. That is why the Divine Savior gave us Confession, the sacrament of Penance, which repairs all damage resulting from sin if we are sorry for the wrong we have done and anxious not to repeat it."

I took a breath and pushed on. "Promise me," I pleaded, "that you will get to Confession here or in another church before next Sunday." Then, on the spur of the moment, without having intended to say anything of the sort, I added, "And promise me too that you will do this every New Year's as long as you live, whether you are in serious need of Confession or not."

The congregation was virtually 100 percent African-American. All of a sudden, promises were being made out loud on every side. As I returned to the altar, I was smiling from cheek to cheek.

Repairs and Resolutions

Some months later, I was given a new priestly assignment. On my last Sunday in the parish, a good-bye reception was held in the school hall. The chair of the parish council presented me with a handsome violet stole, the kind that priests wear in the confessional. "It's for a shepherd who likes to repair broken Magi for his people," he remarked with a wink, "and makes great New Year's resolutions for them, too."

After that, I have had only one New Year's resolution to suggest. Nor do I expect that I will ever have another.

New York, January 2009

Music Lesson

The procession had formed in the vestibule of Saint Aloysius Church in New Canaan, Connecticut. It was the last Sunday in June, and I was beginning an all-day visitation of the parish. There was to be a Mass in the morning, followed by a lunch with the clergy and the parish council at one o'clock, a parish reception in the afternoon, and a second Mass in the evening. I was looking forward to the entire program with genuine delight.

A choir of men and women was assembled on the left of the sanctuary as we looked up the aisle toward the altar. When the pastor gave the signal, the choir director raised his baton. Immediately, the church was engulfed in the powerful strains of Edward Elgar's *Ecce Sacerdos*.

The Elgar, however, was just a hint of what was to come. The Mass was by Mozart and was enhanced with Gregorian Chant and classical polyphony, and the congregation was clearly enthralled.

I, for my part, was not only enthralled but also curiously carried back in memory to the choir of the parish of my boyhood, Saint Giles in Oak Park, Illinois.

❧

The choir director at Saint Giles in the 1940s was Dr. Otto Singenberger. He was an outstanding musician and the son of a noted composer, Sir John Singenberger, the founder of the Caecilian Society, a celebrated organization of church musicians mostly in Europe but also in the Americas.

Dr. Singenberger had been the first choir director of the major seminary of the Archdiocese of Chicago before he came to our parish in Oak Park. I have no idea how old he was when I sang in his choir. To a boy of eight or nine, he, of course, seemed to be well advanced in years.

Three mornings a week, we choir boys from the parish school missed recess and practiced under Dr. Singenberger's direction for forty-five minutes. On Friday evenings we were joined for a two-hour session by twelve tenors and basses and, on very special occasions, by a small group of instrumentalists as well. Finally, on Sunday mornings we all practiced for a half hour before the Solemn High Mass at noon.

Our repertoire was largely German and Italian. We sang compositions of Bach, Mozart, Bruckner, and Rheinberger along with others of Perosi, Refice, Rossini, and Montani. And we sang them all quite well thanks to the considerable musical gifts of Dr. Singenberger and the remarkable ability of a dedicated curate to maintain order among forty or so youngsters between the ages of eight and twelve.

To this day I can still sing by heart the alto part of Perosi's *Missa Pontificalis*, Rossini's *Stabat Mater*, and Bruckner's *Ave Maria*. For this, and especially for the love of sacred music that was instilled in me as a choir boy, I give thanks to the Lord.

That, however, for which I am most grateful in this connection is something quite apart from the music itself.

Before the liturgical reforms of the Second Vatican Council, the Sanctus and Benedictus of the Mass, that is, the "Holy, holy, holy" and the "Blessed is he who comes in the name of the Lord" were sung separately—the Sanctus after the Preface, and the Benedictus after the Consecration.

In those days, when the choir would file into its place in the pews behind the lofty altar of our parish church, we would find Dr. Singenberger at the organ playing the processional and, once we started singing, directing as well. He remained at the organ until the Sanctus, at which time he would lift himself off the organ bench and lower himself onto the floor with arthritic pain clearly evident in his movement and deeply etched in his face. There he would kneel facing the back of the altar until after the Consecration, his head bowed in prayer. He would then return to the organ bench, direct and accompany the Benedictus, and repeat the painful descent, sinking once again to his knees and remaining there until the priest intoned the Our Father.

Even as a child I would think to myself as I watched this spectacle Sunday after Sunday, "Stay there on the organ bench, Dr. Singenberger. You are in so much pain. The Lord will understand. Please stay where you are."

But stay he never did. The Son of God had come upon the altar of our parish church—Body, Blood, Soul, and Divinity. The son of Sir John Singenberger would kneel in adoration, no matter what.

I had learned about the Real Presence of our Blessed Lord in the Eucharist from conversations with my parents, from religion lessons with the Sisters, and from catechism classes with our parish priests. Years later I studied the matter again on the college level and in the seminary. Yet none of these experiences drove the doctrine home as tellingly as the actions of the determined choir director of my boyhood. He knew with unquestioning faith that his Savior was on the altar under the appearances of bread and wine, and without speaking a word, delivered a discourse on the theology of the Eucharist that none, not even children, could fail to grasp.

⸙

The evening liturgy at Saint Aloysius featured a folk Mass in which both the young and the not-so-young participated with devotion and manifest pleasure. The music was well prepared and from the heart.

When we came to the moment of the Consecration, I raised the host, genuflected, raised the chalice, genuflected again, and found my prayer focused on the spiritual well-being of the People of God of Saint Aloysius Parish and—I must confess—on Dr. Otto Singenberger, too.

I imagined that my erstwhile choir director was, from his place in Heaven, watching one of his former choir boys bringing the Son of God down upon the altar of a parish not unlike the one in which he had served for many years. He moves his right hand briskly as though conducting the Mozart and the Elgar, and he attentively follows the unfamiliar rhythms and cadences of the folk Mass. He prays that Church musicians understand that their music is to be inspiring, of course, but that their lives are to be inspiring as well.

He wants to cry out for all to hear that music in the house of the Lord is not just to be excellently sung or played. It is also to be prayed and, above all, *lived* in union with the God Whose glory it is meant to reflect and celebrate.

Bridgeport, September 1991

The Clerk's Advice

The man who directed the Diocesan Office for Youth Activities eight years ago was quite emphatic. "The committee for this year's youth rally wants you to speak to our young people about heavy metal music," he told me. "It would mean a lot to all of us if you could do it."

"I know nothing about heavy metal music," I observed. "Try to find someone else. I would much prefer another topic."

"Please," he countered. "The committee is unanimous. This is the kind of music that our kids are listening to. They should know what you think of it."

The next day my priest-secretary and I visited a music store in one of the local shopping malls.

"Which heavy metal tapes are you selling the most of these days?" I asked a male clerk of about twenty years of age. He gestured toward a cardboard display case entitled "Heavy Metal — The Top Ten."

My secretary chose four tapes and set them on the counter.

"Aren't you Bishop Egan?" the clerk inquired.

"Yes," I answered.

"Well then, I don't think you want these," the clerk announced, pulling the tapes toward himself. "They are pretty rough. Actually, worse than rough. They're not for you."

"I think I can handle them," I said. "I need them for a talk I have been asked to give."

"Choose something else," the clerk insisted. "This is definitely not the kind of thing you have in mind." He gathered up the tapes to put them back in the display case.

"I have to take them," I announced. "I have no choice."

That evening, alone in my home, I had my introduction to what many of the young people of our nation were hearing day after day. It was difficult to understand all the words because of the drumming and shouting in the background.

However, inside each of the plastic cases containing the tapes there was a tightly folded sheet of paper about twelve inches long and four inches high. It contained the lyrics to each of the songs, lyrics that were outrageous beyond all imagining. Violence, casual and twisted sex, drugs, and the mistreatment of women were the constant themes. I suddenly realized how out of touch I had been.

"How did we ever sink to this?" I asked myself. "When did all of this nastiness take over?"

The youth rally, which was held in Danbury, Connecticut, was very well attended. There were workshops on a number of interesting and inspiring subjects in the morning. There was a beautiful Mass at noon before lunch. There were games in the afternoon, and there was a general meeting to close the day with the bishop as the speaker.

I had promised myself not to sound like Moses coming down from the mountain, although this was clearly my first inclination. I would be calm, understanding, and reasonable, I told myself. I would report what I had heard on the tapes and point out the evils they were fostering, and I would do my best to win the audience to my point of view.

Yes, calm, understanding, and reasonable—these would be the hallmarks of my presentation.

When the talk concluded, the young people were eager to have their say.

"Sure, this stuff is pretty gross," one tall teenager in baggy jeans conceded. "But we don't take it seriously. In fact, most of us don't even know the words the heavy metal groups are singing."

A groan of disagreement went up from the crowd, and another teenager in even baggier jeans raised his hand. "Some of us know the words pretty well," he declared.

"What about the song I mentioned just before the question period? Do you recall its words?" I asked.

"Sure enough," he responded; and he started to recite them aloud by heart. Several joined in until it began to strike everyone how sick and ugly the song was. Slowly, the recitation lost steam, and silence ensued.

I ended my remarks with more emotion than I had intended. Calm, understanding, and reasonable were somehow lost in the fray. I begged my audience to recognize how degrading much of this music was. I assured them that I was once a teenager and that I knew how important it is for teenagers to be "with it," "cool," and such.

"Still," I pleaded, "think this through. Think it through with your parents, guardians, and grandparents. There are times in life when we do well to be out of style. There are times in life when swimming against the current is the only healthy and worthy course."

The audience appeared to be more sympathetic than I had expected. Indeed, out of nowhere groups started to applaud. I immediately began a closing prayer; and as I surveyed the crowd, I found several with their eyes closed and even a few with their hands folded. I dared to suspect that the Lord may have allowed me to do some little good.

⌒

Eight years later, and only a few weeks ago, I was sitting on the edge of my bed at eleven o'clock in the evening, having just returned home from a Confirmation. Out of habit, I switched on the television. As the tube adjusted itself, a deep voice emerged. It was discussing the recent tragic events in Littleton, Colorado,[1] and the concern of parents and teachers about the music to which our teenagers are listening and the videos they are watching.

"When all is said and done," the voice proclaimed in a tone of disdain, "it is pointless and even a bit silly to criticize what the American entertainment industry is providing our young people today on tapes and screens." It has never been "scientifically proved," the voice continued, "to cause any serious damage." The song lyrics, for example, that certain "mean-spirited groups" find offensive have little effect on youthful minds. Of course, some performers "go to extremes." But we are a nation committed to "freedom of artistic expression." It is up to our children to make "critical judgments" about what they choose to see and hear, and we adults are well advised not to "interfere."

The man behind the voice was elegantly dressed. He spoke with an air of authority, and no one on the panel of which he was a part dared to challenge him with more than a raised eyebrow.

---

[1] At Columbine High School on April 20, 1999, two student gunmen killed thirteen and wounded twenty-one.

At first I was angry; but soon my anger melted into sadness — sadness for the bumptious speaker and sadness especially for the youth of our nation.

~

The following Friday evening, I was scheduled for one of the most delightful events on my calendar — the annual awards ceremony for Cub Scouts, Boy Scouts, Girl Scouts, and Campfire Girls. It takes place in the Cathedral of Saint Augustine, and this year the crowd was the largest ever.

Banners led us up the aisle. The Pledge of Allegiance was recited. Prayers followed. A passage was read from the Epistle of Saint Paul to the Romans. I delivered a brief sermon to the youngsters and, one by one, they came forward to receive their medals with fathers, mothers, brothers, sisters, grandparents, and family friends applauding, cheering, and taking pictures.

Here is healthy, wholesome America, I mused to myself, as I shook hand after hand and posed for photograph after photograph. The elegant gentleman on the television panel and those whom he represents will very likely remain in control of our media, our movies, and our music for many years to come.

Still, there is hope, and the reason is families — families like the ones proudly and lovingly celebrating the achievements of their children here in the Cathedral of Saint Augustine.

If parents, guardians, and grandparents stay close to our youth, if they are readily available for conversation and direction about popular music and all other factors significantly influencing the lives of young people today, we can and we will find our way through the troubled and often frightening cultural milieu in which we live. There are no other safeguards, there are no other sure defenses, and perhaps we should not be surprised.

Practice for Heaven

For this is the way the Lord has made us. We are images of a loving and caring God Who meant us to live, mature, and be formed physically, psychologically, and morally in loving and caring families. When society is turned upside down, it is the family that uniquely can and clearly must set it aright.

"I don't think you want these. They're not for you. Choose something else," the young clerk in the music store counseled the aging bishop.

May the concern and guidance of our parents, guardians, and grandparents be no less wise and, above all, no less insistent.

Bridgeport, June 1999

Altars Are Meant to Make Us Strong

It was the summer of 1940. The nation was preoccupied with a raging war in Europe and a fearsome epidemic of poliomyelitis from the Atlantic to the Pacific. I was one of the victims of the epidemic. After I had spent three weeks in the Cook County Contagious Disease Hospital, the medical authorities allowed my family to take me home.

In my bedroom, atop a chest of drawers, was a small plaster altar that had been given to me by one of my many aunts. It was white with a green and gold angel on either side of the taber-nacle and a bas-relief of Da Vinci's *Last Supper* on the front of the altar itself. On top of the tabernacle stood a crucifix and six candles — three on each side — that glowed when the altar was plugged in, thanks to a lightbulb hidden inside.

For the first seven or eight months of my convalescence, a doctor came to our house once a week, sent by the local health authorities in cooperation with the March of Dimes. He was a young man with a large moustache, and his visits followed a pattern. I would be taken out of the "Sister Kenny packs"[2] of

---

[2] Elizabeth Kenny (1880–1952) was an Australian nurse ("sister") who pioneered an unconventional approach to the treatment of polio. Instead of immobilization with braces and casts, Sister

hot, wet wool in which I spent my days to be carefully examined. The doctor would then put one hand behind my neck and the other under my legs and, cradling me, see how high my head and shoulders could be raised.

Although I was eight years old, I must confess that I often cried rather angrily, not because of the pain, but because of the seeming hopelessness of it all. After several months, I still could not be pulled into a sitting position, much less sit up on my own.

One day, when I was behaving particularly badly, the doctor gave me a lecture, the theme of which was that only courageous people contract polio. His argument centered on the president of the United States who was then in office, Franklin Delano Roosevelt, and others whose names I no longer recall. It was evidently clear that I was not much impressed. So the doctor sat silently for a while, rose, went over to the chest of drawers, bent down, and plugged in the altar.

"Altars are meant to make us strong," he announced. And, with that, he launched into a rather involved theological disquisition. I well remember three of the points that he made. First, Jesus Christ suffered and died on the altar of the Cross to make us spiritually strong. Second, it was time for me to stop feeling sorry for myself and start getting strong spiritually and physically, too.

And, third—and most importantly—the way to do this was to focus my attention on the altar in my bedroom, with its six glowing candles and the Lord on His Cross, the Lord Who was waiting for me to join my sufferings to His.

Kenny favored muscle stimulation through hot compresses and intensive physiotherapy.

⁀

The doctor continued to come for his weekly visits. There were, however, no more sermons, just as there was no more crying or whining. All the same, on several occasions before leaving, he would give me a quick, knowing smile, go over to the plaster altar, bend down, and plug it in.

About a year and a half later, I was up and getting around reasonably well. Once a week, I went to a physiotherapist in a neighboring town for exercises, first in warm water and then on a gymnast's mat.

One afternoon, as I was getting back into my clothes, the young doctor with the large moustache appeared. "How's our altar?" he inquired. I hated to tell him that my older brother had attempted to replace the lightbulb inside and shattered the altar in the process, but I did.

"Maybe that's just as well," the doctor observed. "It's probably time for you to graduate to real altars."

I said nothing, but he went on. "As I once told you," he said, "altars are meant to make us strong. For the rest of your life, when things are going badly and you feel you cannot handle it, look for an altar, and put your sufferings on it next to those of your Lord and Savior. Together, you and He will find the strength to do whatever needs to be done."

⁀

Fifty years later, I was sent an obituary from the *Chicago Tribune*. The doctor had passed away, honored by medical societies in the United States and Canada.

I felt terrible. How I wished that I had contacted him before he died to tell him of my gratitude for his medical care and, especially, for his having taken the time to speak to me about altars. How I wished I had been able to let him know that, with each passing year, I came to understand better what he had evidently understood quite early in his life — that altars are meant to make us strong.

Bridgeport, August 1989

And Now a Word from Our Mothers

One of our archdiocesan priests had taken a turn for the worse in a hospital where he had been for some weeks. He was on my mind throughout a Mass that I was celebrating for the Latino community at Cardinal Spellman High School in the Bronx. At the bidding prayers, I asked the congregation to pray for the priest, and after the Mass, I left immediately for the hospital.

The man at the information desk directed me to the ICU (intensive care unit), on the fourth floor. As I emerged from the elevator, I spied a sign on the opposite wall telling me to go into a waiting room, dial a certain number on the telephone, indicate the patient I wanted to visit, and be seated until someone came to get me. All of this I did, relieved to know that the priest was still among the living.

There was only one other person in the waiting room. She was an African-American woman of perhaps thirty-five years of age. Seated at a tiny table, she was eating her dinner from a cardboard container.

A television set attached to the wall high over our heads was showing a situation comedy in which the parents of the house-wife were having dinner with their daughter, their son-in-law, and two children. An argument ensued, and the father-in-law leaned into the camera to call the son-in-law a name that was both blasphemous and unclean.

The canned laughter was raised to an unusually high level. When it subsided, the woman in the room with me announced angrily: "They want to wreck our kids with all this ugliness and filth. That's why they show this stuff at suppertime. But, I won't let them wreck mine. No, you can count on that. I won't let them."

I had no chance to respond, if a response was desired. For the telephone rang; and before either of us could answer it, a nurse appeared at the waiting room door to signal the woman to follow her into the ICU. She rose, went over to a receptacle in the corner, deposited her cardboard container, and turned to me to repeat with a certain solemnity, "I won't let them."

In due course, my time came to enter the ICU to look for the priest I had come to see. He was very sick and did not respond to my greeting or my questions. Thus, I leaned in toward him to recite prayers as loud as I dared over the blare of the six o'clock news that was being transmitted on a television set above his bed. After giving him my blessing, I went to look for the woman from the waiting room to offer her a word of encouragement. She was nowhere to be found.

Still, she remained on my mind for several days afterward. Indeed, one evening at a charity dinner, I told two couples sitting with me of my experience in the hospital, confessing that I was not sure what I would have said to the woman if I had found her.

One of my table partners, a mother of several and a grandmother of several more, cleared her throat, waited until she had the attention of us all, and enunciated her "five basic rules" for dealing with "bad TV, radio, movies, magazines, and the songs youngsters listen to with those little loops in their ears." Her "rules" struck me as marvelously wise.

Here they are in my words. They were much more powerful in hers. Hence, I will fit in hers, to the extent that I can remember them.

1. Be in charge as regards the television. Have the set in a room where everyone can watch it, and have it turned off when what is being shown is "violent or off-color."

2. When what was seen was unacceptable, sit down and discuss it openly and thoroughly. "Don't be afraid. Children need to know you can handle this sort of thing."

3. As long as youngsters are in high school, make sure you know what movies they are going to see, what magazines they are buying and reading, and what they are hearing on "the newfangled radio devices." "And again, don't be afraid. Deep down, children want boundaries, reasonable boundaries, boundaries that show you really and truly care about them."

4. Eat together and see to it that everyone has a chance to "say his or her piece." The dinner table is the best classroom for the lessons children need to learn. Nothing will ever take its place.

5. Pray. The recitation of even one decade of the Rosary by parents and children together after dinner is the most powerful defense against whatever damage may be done by the communications media. Prayer puts life into focus, and family prayer will always be remembered with gratitude and love.

Practice for Heaven

A voice came over the loudspeaker calling us to order so that the persons to be honored at the dinner might come forward to receive their awards. The husband of the "rule giver" patted her on the hand. "Well put," he said.

She smiled and winked at me. "He usually doesn't like my sermons," she claimed.

"I like that one," he retorted. "Some of the others, Cardinal, still need work. But not that one."

At home after the dinner, I scanned the morning newspapers before turning in. One of them featured an article about contract negotiations that writers for television, motion pictures, and radio had just entered with movie producers and station owners. According to the article, preliminary statements by both sides were "tough and hard-hitting."

What a great idea it would be, I mused to myself, if the two mothers of my recent acquaintance could join those talks. They would have something of inestimable value to add about what the writers for television, motion pictures, and radio; movie producers; and station owners are doing to our youth — and to all of us, for that matter.

"Tough and hard-hitting" might be ennobled by "strong and wise." And, if all were listening in good faith, the result could be "human and decent."

New York, November 2007

Keeping the Faith "Wrightly"

Public television in July of this year aired a two-part series on the life and work of Frank Lloyd Wright, who died in 1959 at the age of ninety, and, according to the *Encyclopaedia Britannica*, "won more honors at home and abroad than any other architect of his time." I was able to view only part 1 of the series. All the same, for reasons that are quite personal, what I saw left a deep impression.

Almost half of the presentation concerned twenty-six homes that Wright had designed in the Village of Oak Park, Illinois, where I was born and reared. The homes are all well known to me. In fact, for two years I studied music in one of them every Thursday afternoon. My teacher had purchased the place in the late 1930s, primarily because the living room was spacious enough to host two concert grand pianos and thirty to forty guests for recitals.

⟳

On Thursdays I would arrive at the appointed time, music in hand, usually to wait an hour or more in one of the parlors that led into the living room. My teacher had a keen sense of rhythm but no sense whatever of time. All of my fellow students had learned to wait patiently for their lessons, never daring to complain.

Thus it was that I passed many hours in rooms designed by Frank Lloyd Wright, on occasion trying to peer through the stained-glass windows for which he was famous when I heard an unexpected noise out on the street, but usually just squirming rather uncomfortably in the high-back chairs and built-in benches with which Wright furnished his Oak Park creations.

I knew full well that my teacher's home was by Wright, as were three others on the same block. I knew that Wright enjoyed a formidable reputation in the world of architecture. Indeed, I often paged through a collection of highly flattering books about him that were stowed in shelves that formed the usual doorway to the dining room of the home.

Still, I do not recall ever being much taken by the place. The Mozart, the Chopin, and the Ravel that I was studying there touched me as deeply as great art can touch a child of ten or eleven. For I was being schooled in them by someone who loved them passionately and earnestly strived to share them with others. But the architecture that was the setting of the music lessons—it left no mark whatever.

No mark, that is, until I happened to view the aforementioned television presentation. As the camera moved about almost devoutly through several of the Oak Park homes, I began to realize what a master of space, form, light, and even drama Frank Lloyd Wright was, thanks to the author of the narration, who was clearly enthralled by his subject. Hence, more than half a century after my rather casual introduction to the art of the man who had "won more honors at home and abroad than any other architect of his time," I was beginning to rejoice in his genius.

Keeping the Faith "Wrightly"

With apologies to the redoubtable Yogi Berra, the experience was a kind of *déjà vu* in reverse.

⁓

Less than a week after the screening of the television program, a woman wrote to seek my counsel. She and her husband, she reported, had been Catholics all of their lives. They belonged, in her words, to "that generation of people who learned their *Baltimore Catechism* by heart and knew their Faith well." Nonetheless, she confessed, that faith seemed to be slipping away from them both.

"It just isn't *doing it* anymore, Bishop," she complained. "Where are we old-time Catholics to find the old fire?"

My reply was not complicated. Faith, I explained, is an unearned gift from God. It can, however, wane and even disappear if it is not cared for properly.

The *Baltimore Catechism* gave us "old-timers" a great start. Its questions and answers were marvelously clear. They zeroed in on the essentials of what we followers of Jesus Christ believe, and in their time they were highly effective largely because of the manner in which most Catholics were then living their lives in family and parish.

The times, however, have changed. The supports of the Faith that once came from home and Church are weakening in many quarters. Moreover, the cinema, the television, and the news media are now often openly hostile to the Church and her teachings; and the same is in large measure true of academe and many sectors of government.

Thus, to keep the fire of belief alive, we need to be regularly and powerfully inspired by those who love it and strive to share it.

When I was a youngster, the music of Mozart, Chopin, and Ravel meant a great deal to me, while the architecture of Wright meant little or nothing. The reason, of course, was obvious: I had someone to bring me to appreciate the former and no one to do the same as regards to the latter. A leader, a guide, a teacher was wanting.

And who is to fulfill this function for us believers of today?

In my estimate, the saints, first and foremost. We, I would submit, need to acquire the habit of studying — or, better, of listening to — the heroes and heroines of the Faith, both in what they have written and especially in how they have lived. Physicists concern themselves with matter and motion, and with Newton and Einstein as well. Lawyers concern themselves with contracts and torts, and with Blackstone and Holmes as well. Painters concern themselves with forms and colors, and with Michelangelo and Monet as well.

We who seek to tighten our grip on revelation will wisely follow suit. Francis of Assisi and Catherine of Siena, Thomas Aquinas and Thérèse of Lisieux, Damien of Molokai and Frances Xavier Cabrini of New York and Chicago have much to teach us. If these "experts in the Faith" are but granted a hearing, their pens and their deeds can fire up even the weakest embers of belief.

Similarly, those who truly yearn to embrace all that the Lord has revealed require, along with the inspiration of the saints, the guidance and assistance of directors of retreats and days of recollection. No one masters the arts or sciences alone. Hence, in every period of history, ours included, mentors, tutors, trainers, counselors, coaches, and even gurus abound; and all the world concedes how necessary they are.

In the art and science of belief the same holds true. We urgently need to listen to others who are deeply committed to the

Faith as they explain it and exult in it, if we are to maintain it and treasure it. Retreats and days of recollection, with competent and dedicated directors, answer that need mightily.

Finally, I would mention three other groups to assist us in firming up our beliefs. They are:

- lecturers and discussion leaders in courses of adult education in parishes and other religious institutions
- friends who come together in the Lord for formal study of Scripture, Tradition, and Church teaching
- coworkers in undertakings of justice and charity who are willing to speak and pray with us about what we are doing together and why

All of these will surely light the old fire, if given a chance.

∾

In the back of one of my bookcases I recently discovered a volume that I had long since forgotten. Its title is *The Genius of Frank Lloyd Wright*, and its final pages focus on another of Wright's masterworks in my hometown, a church he designed for Lake Street, the main thoroughfare.

The most important facet of the building, according to the book's author, is the placement of the pulpit. It is not above the congregation or off to one side. Rather, it juts right into the middle of the front pews on ground level so that "immediate and intimate communication" might be achieved between the preacher and the faithful.

Wright belonged to "no established church," according to the narrator of the public-television presentation. Whatever of this, I suspect he might have understood the needs of believers rather well. For he brought them as close as he could to their teachers and guides.

Acceptance of the Faith comes from hearing those who themselves firmly believe, Saint Paul tells us in his epistle to the Romans (10:17). The same, we insist, applies to holding on to it.

Bridgeport, September 1999

Signed and Sealed

There is in London a bookseller by the name of Paul Slennett who worries over the moral and religious state of the United Kingdom. Last March, Mr. Slennett decided to do something about his concerns. Accordingly, he put together $88,500 and approached the British Postal Service with the request that, for two months, April and May of 1988, each and every card and letter mailed in England, Wales, Scotland, and Northern Ireland be sealed with a postmark consisting of a cross and the words "Jesus Is Alive."

Since 1917, in order to bolster revenues, the British government had been allowing the purchase of postmarks and never had the practice occasioned upset. However, when Mr. Slennett's message began appearing on correspondence, the roar went up. Newspapers were besieged with letters to the editor full of angry protests. In fact, the National Secular Society of Great Britain announced that it would soon be taking up a collection "among atheists and agnostics" for a postmark that would read: "Jesus Is a Myth."

On this side of the ocean, Mr. Slennett's undertaking met mostly with humor. *Newsweek* attempted to evoke a smile by writing, "It's enough to drive a non-believer around the bend";

and *Time* told the story under the title "Onward Christian Postage."

⁓

Nevertheless, the mail went out; and for two months, over a billion cards and letters bore a seal that proclaimed to those with whom the English, Welsh, Scots, and Northern Irish were corresponding that "Jesus Is Alive."

What effect Mr. Slennett might have had on morals and religion in the United Kingdom is anyone's guess. Undoubtedly, many were moved at least to think, and perhaps even to talk about, the Lord, His reality, His vitality. And that, evidently, is all to the good. Still, it is difficult to assume that much more than this was achieved.

There is, however, another kind of sealing with a similar message that will be taking place in the Diocese of Bridgeport beginning this March, and continuing on through April and May. It will be done by Bishop Curtis[3] and myself, and it will leave its mark, not on cards and letters, but on foreheads and hearts.

I refer, of course, to the sealing that happens when the sacrament of Confirmation is conferred.

Traditionally, Confirmation has been understood in terms of courage, fortitude, and strength. It is that sacrament, we learn from the *Catechism*, that "makes us strong, dedicated Christians and soldiers of Christ." It is because of that sacrament that we are to "profess and practice our Faith openly, never be ashamed

---

[3] Walter W. Curtis (1913–1997) was bishop of the Diocese of Bridgeport from 1961 to 1988, when he was retired and succeeded by then-Bishop Egan.

of it, and die rather than deny it" (cf. *Baltimore Catechism*, nos. 670, 686).

⁀

All of this is both inspiring and true. However, with the Second Vatican Council, the element of witness on the part of the confirmed has come to be emphasized first and foremost. The Fathers of the Council highlighted, especially in *Lumen Gentium*, their Dogmatic Constitution on the Church (no. 33), that Confirmation is to make us givers of testimony by word and deed to all the Lord has revealed. With its emphasis on the universal call to holiness, the Second Vatican Council reminded the laity that they are called upon as living members to expend all their energy for the growth of the Church and its continuous sanctification. The lay apostolate, therefore, is a participation in the saving mission of the Church itself. Through their Baptism and Confirmation, all are commissioned to that apostolate by the Lord Himself.

Confirmation seals us with a message the world needs to hear, a message that is rather well summed up by the Cross and the words Paul Slennett had imprinted on British mail: "Jesus Is Alive."

Strong Christians, yes, but witnessing Christians as well: it is this for which the bishop prays when he makes the Sign of the Cross on the forehead of the one to be confirmed and says: "Be sealed with the gift of the Holy Spirit." He is asking the Lord to make of the confirmed an announcer of salvation in Jesus Christ, an announcer whom the world will not be able to ignore.

What would happen if, this spring, the thousands — yes, thousands — who are to be confirmed here in Fairfield County were to leave their parish churches and march into the world as people of honor who never betray the truth; people of justice who never deny others their rights; people of purity who never forget they are images of divinity; people of charity who never turn their backs on those in need; people of prayer who never think of themselves as being out of the presence of their Creator?

What would happen? The world would stand up, take notice, and ask why. And the world would both hear the testimony and, to use the modern parlance, get the message.

∽

As it turned out, the National Secular Society of Great Britain did not take up its collection. Hence, thus far only Paul Slennett has had his say.

We wait to hear from those who are to be confirmed during the coming months here in the Diocese of Bridgeport, indeed, from all in the diocese who have been confirmed. They know the Lord, His life, and His Cross. Signed with that Cross and sealed with the oil of Confirmation, they can by the witness of their lives tell the world most effectively what it yearns above all else to be told: that Jesus is alive.

And, this is precisely what they are called to do.

Onward, Christian witnesses. You have been signed and sealed.

Bridgeport, April 1989

Master Catechists

Bogotá, Colombia, is blessed with scores of magnificent churches. One moves about the town enthralled by the size and elegance of one after another. A bishop friend and I stood one August in a plaza resplendent with flowers of all kinds, gazing at the magnificently carved façade of another imposing Spanish-style house of God.

As we entered, our attention was immediately drawn to the main altar at the top of the center aisle and the huge gilded reredos that rose behind it. The scene was nothing short of breathtaking as beams from the early-morning sun played upon the countless rows of delicately sculptured saints and angels populating the reredos from floor to ceiling.

My companion moved toward the main altar to photograph it. I, instead, made my way over to the side of the church, having noticed that, at the end of the right aisle, there was no altar or shrine, but rather a stone platform dominated by a towering arch under which one might suspect that an altar and its reredos were once to be found.

On the platform stood a woman of perhaps thirty-five years of age, in front of a black metal stand six or seven feet high. Draped over the stand was a bundle of colorful posters clipped together, which an elderly gentleman manipulated at the direction of the woman. Around the woman, the elderly gentleman, and the poster stand, fifty to sixty children were seated on little wooden chairs, and to the right of them about the same number of adults, all listening with rapt attention to what the woman was saying.

"Who is she?" I inquired of a teenage boy who happened to be standing near me.

"*Una catequista* [a catechist]," he replied with a look that registered surprise at my ignorance.

～

I mounted the stone platform, and took my place behind the adults, to the left of the catechist. She was telling her charges about the seven sacraments and had posters to illustrate each of them. The sacrament under consideration when I joined the group was Confirmation. The first poster showed, in the foreground, a bishop anointing the forehead of a young man and, in the background, the descent of the Holy Spirit upon Mary and the Apostles.

What the catechist had to say was classic catechetical material expressed in classic catechetical formulae. What made her presentation so gripping, however, was her teaching style. She moved gracefully in among the children, her eyes filled with excitement and her voice as clear as a silver bell. Every so often, she would bend from the waist before a youngster to gain his attention and then glide back to the poster stand, gesturing at times vigorously and at times almost in slow motion.

When the section on Confirmation was completed, the catechist took her place in front of the poster stand, her feet together, her hands folded, and her eyes cast down.

"Now," said she, "it is time for our Blessed Lord to speak to each of us about the sacrament of Confirmation. Close your eyes, fold your hands, and listen."

We all did as directed, boys and girls, men and women. I had been keenly aware of the loud talking and constant shuffling of feet in the center aisle of the church and also of the unrelenting street noise that was wafting in through the open windows. Yet, none of this seemed to intrude upon the altogether uncanny atmosphere of prayer in which we were suddenly engulfed. The Master Catechist, from His throne in Heaven, had taken over from the master catechist standing before us. There was not a sound to be heard from a hundred or more persons of various ages who, with eyes closed and hands folded, were giving the same attention to the second section of the catechism lesson as they had given to the first.

⌒

The elderly gentleman carefully turned to the posters that had to do with the sacrament of Reconciliation, or Penance. The catechist called us to order, and a new lesson was under way.

I moved in closer, placing myself immediately behind the children in the little wooden chairs. This proved to be a mistake. For, during the Lord's part of the lesson on the sacrament of Confirmation, my camera case came undone, and out spilled three plastic containers of film that bounced over the stone pavement with an eerie, hollow sound that caught the attention of all. Two men bent to pick up the containers, their heads met, and the children broke into howls of laughter.

"*Lo siento, lo siento* [I am sorry, I am sorry]," I told the catechist rather too loudly and in my embarrassment dropped the film containers again.

The catechist, bubbling with laughter, observed that the visitor from the United States was clearly penitent and that he was absolved as well. With that, she dismissed the class, announcing she would be back in her place for another lesson at 4:30 in the afternoon.

≈

On page 336 of my Fodor's guidebook of South America, just above the section entitled "Exploring Bogotá," I entered an account of my adventure. It read as follows:

> Attended a morning catechism class here, given by a marvelous woman and the Lord. I interrupted what the Lord was saying about the sacrament of Confirmation and felt terrible. The woman and the Lord will be back in the afternoon, and so will I.

Bridgeport, November 1991

A Priest's Life

Criticism, ridicule, rejection and worse can be the price one pays for daring to take stands "in true righteousness and holiness" (Ephesians 4:24). And the price mounts when one invites others to do the same. Nonetheless, this is part and parcel of what the priestly calling must entail, and when it does, priesthood is complete.

Sacrifice — and Much More

Some weeks ago, the editor of *Catholic New York* asked me to write an article about what being a priest means to me. I agreed with some hesitation, since the priesthood is something very precious and personal for me. I would not want to diminish it with uncareful or, worse yet, self-serving words. All the same, here is my attempt to do what I was asked to do.

For me, what defines a priest is sacrifice in two senses of that word. The first and essential of these two senses is a matter of prayer. I have always considered sacrifice — the offering of something of value to God as an expression of worship — as the zenith of prayer. It has been so for eons in every corner of the world where human beings have sought to adore, thank, and seek forgiveness, blessings, and protection from their God.

On the Cross, the Son of God made Man, Jesus Christ, our Lord and Savior, sacrificed Himself in an act of obedient worship that surpassed all sacrifices of all times. He was the Priest. He was the Victim. And He left no doubt about this whatever; for example, when, in His discourse on being the Good Shepherd, He declared: "I lay down my life in order to take it up again. No one takes it from me, but I lay it down of my own accord" (John 10:17–18).

Practice for Heaven

In the Holy Sacrifice of the Mass, what transpired on Calvary's Cross is a reality once again in an unbloody manner. Jesus Christ is the Priest. Jesus Christ is the Victim. However, just as the Victim is present under the appearances of bread and wine, so the Priest — the Eternal High Priest — is present in the person of the ordained priest who stands at the altar as an instrument in the hands of the Savior.

For me, this is the priesthood in its essence. This is what defines a priest of the New Covenant. All else in my understanding of that to which I have been called must fall into place under this rubric. I am the one who, in the most intimate union with Jesus Christ, offers the Sacrifice of Sacrifices, the prayer of prayers, the Holy Sacrifice of the Mass.

⁀

There is, however, a second sense of sacrifice in the life of a priest. In the providence of an all-loving God, no one can be a worthy, faithful priest of Jesus Christ unless he is willing, in a genuine spirit of sacrifice, to deny himself whatever is not in accord with priestly service and generously give himself to doing all that such service requires. I view celibacy in the Latin Rite of the one, holy, catholic, and apostolic Church in this light, just as I view in the same light all demands — whether heavy or light — that emerge as one lives out one's life as a priest.

For a man to be an authentic, effective priest, sacrifice in both senses must be operative — the sacrifice of the Cross at the altar and the sacrifices that priestly life inevitably imposes day by day.

When I am asked about the meaning of priesthood, I start with sacrifice.

But there is more.

To be a priest who serves his God and the People of God as they are to be served, one must be deeply committed to preaching the mind and will of God as revealed "in season and out of season" (see 2 Tim. 4:1–5). Nor is this a duty free of challenges. It requires attentive study of Scripture, Tradition, and the teachings of the Church; prayerful meditation on them all; and assiduous preparation of what is to be said about them and how it is to be said. There are no shortcuts, and making one's peace with this reality is an expression of priestly self-sacrifice.

Moreover, the priestly preacher must always be honest with his people. His calling is to announce what has been made known for our salvation. He is to add nothing. He is to subtract nothing. He is to repeat revelation whole and entire, with love for what he is repeating and with all the skill he can muster. If sacrifice is a focus of his life and authentic proclamation of what God has revealed is an enthusiastically embraced duty of his life, his priesthood will be a blessing for him and for all whose lives he touches.

Still, there is a third essential element in my understanding of what a priest is and must be. One who stands at the altar in the place of Jesus Christ and stands in the pulpit announcing the gospel of Jesus Christ needs to live the life that Jesus Christ taught us to live and live it without half measures. We all, of course, know what that life is. It is a life of honor, justice, charity, cleanness of heart, and prayer; and we must all live it, whether clerical, religious, or lay.

A priest, however, has a further obligation. He is to lead others to live it as well.

Practice for Heaven

The task is often burdensome. When the fashionable agree that innocent lives can be taken if people "choose" to take them, it is awkward to be out of step. When the powerful insist that the warlike are uniquely patriotic, it is troublesome to dissent. When the comfortable maintain that all is well, it is unwelcome to point to the uncomfortable for whom all is anything but well.

Criticism, ridicule, rejection, and worse can be the price one pays for daring to take stands "true righteousness and holiness" (Ephesians 4:24). And the price mounts when one invites others to do the same. Nonetheless, this is part and parcel of what the priestly calling entails; and when it does, priesthood is complete.

Fifty years ago, when I was ordained in Rome,[4] I committed myself to this understanding of what it means to be a priest. I share it here in the fervent hope that the People of God of the Archdiocese of New York will join me in begging the Savior for a growth of vocations in our midst. At this moment in our history, there is no other need so great.

May the "Lord of the harvest" hear our prayers and answer them abundantly.

New York, December 2007

---

[4] On December 15, 2007, Cardinal Egan celebrated the fiftieth anniversary of his priestly ordination.

The Lord, Saint Martin, and All of Us

The pastor's study was on the second floor of the rectory and looked out on the school playground. When, in 1971, I took over the reins of the parish, which was located on the South Side of Chicago, I used to sit at my desk and enjoy the chatter of the children at play as a kind of musical background.

It was at that desk that I first came to notice a boy from the parish whom I will call Peter. He had been hired by the janitor and the director of religious education for summer work around the parish in a number of capacities. One was supervising the basketball games in the playground. Although he was only four-teen, his authority appeared to be acknowledged by all. From my study window, I would often marvel at his effectiveness, kindness, and youthful wisdom.

My marveling notably increased one warm, humid afternoon when I happened into the parish church and found Peter there catechizing a group of youngsters from the neighborhood. He was seated on the steps leading up to the Communion rail, and the other children were huddled together in the front pews. His theme was devotion to the saints, and his handling of it struck me as not only original but also as quite compelling.

"The Lord has a lot of great friends in Heaven," he explained to his young charges. "They are the saints who want to be our friends, too. Sometimes, when you are talking to the Lord about something you need, it's good to bring a few friends along with you so that they can put in a good word. The saints are there to lend a helping hand. Try it. You'll see that it works."

⁓

I was by no means the only one taken by Peter's maturity and manifest goodness. To save money on fuel and light, I used to celebrate the weekday Masses in a rectory office that had been converted into a kind of chapel. We called it the Chapel of Saint Martin de Porres because it boasted a lovely statue of the saint that had been discovered in a storeroom in the basement of the rectory.

Well over 90 percent of our parishioners were African-American, and they were delighted that Saint Martin, a black man who called himself "the Slave of the Poor," was the patron of the chapel. As a rule, between fifteen and twenty of the most devout of them would come for weekday Mass. They were all good friends, and they were all quite perceptive as well.

On a July morning after Mass, one of their number came to see me. "We think you should speak with Peter about going to the seminary," he said. "We believe he is just the kind of young black man that the Church needs in its city parishes. And we feel he should be ordained as soon as he is old enough."

I had great esteem for the man who had come to speak with me. He was an accountant by profession who kept our finances in order at no cost to the parish. He and his wife were in the rectory at least one night a week while he updated the parish accounts. Early in my tenure, they had become very special friends of mine, and I used to do a good deal of kidding around with them.

"And who is this 'we' of whom you speak?" I asked in a joking tone. My friend fixed his eyes on me with deadly seriousness and replied, "The Lord, Saint Martin, and all of us. That's the 'we.'"

I realized that this was no time for levity and promised to speak with Peter the very next day.

For some reason, I felt awkward about the interview. I did not know the boy well and had no idea how we would handle my proposal. Nonetheless, spurred on by "the Lord, Saint Martin, and all of us," I chatted with him for about a half hour and finally came to the point. "Peter," I asked, "would you like to be a priest?"

The reply was simple and direct, very much in the style I should have expected. "Yes, Father, I would," he answered. "I want to be a missionary in China. Can you help me?"

I have no explicit intelligence about how the Lord and Saint Martin reacted to this response, but I do know that "all of us" were not pleased with Peter's desire to be a missionary in far-away China. Still, the parishioners for the most part made their peace with his choice, and several of them urged me to find a seminary for him.

That fall he entered the minor seminary of the Society of the Divine Word, a missionary congregation. The parish hosted a going-away party at which the director of religious education, a delightful Sister of Providence, cried a bit along with a group of ladies from the Altar and Rosary Society. Our one consolation was that Peter would be a priest somewhere and would be back with us in the summer during his early years of seminary formation.

The following December, I was transferred to Rome. I sent Peter a note with my new address and a promise of prayers. We exchanged cards and letters for several years, but at length lost contact with each other.

Early in August of 1993, while preparing to leave for World Youth Day in Denver, Colorado, I quickly looked through the mail that had come into my office in the Diocese of Bridgeport, where I was the bishop. One letter was from a parish in the Midwest and was signed "Peter." The author was a young man with whom I had discussed the priesthood twenty-two years earlier. He had completed his minor seminary studies, he wrote, and decided he would prefer to work in a parish in the United States. Thus, he had entered a local diocesan seminary, been ordained, completed two assignments as a curate, and was now a pastor.

Some weeks before, he reported, he had met the director of religious education of our old Chicago parish in a nursing home in which she had recently taken up residence. She had insisted that he write to tell me that he was a city pastor, that his parish had an elementary school which he was struggling to keep open, and that he had never thought he could be so happy.

The next day, I celebrated the Votive Mass of Saint Martin de Porres with genuine fervor and joy. I prayed for Peter, for his parish, for his school, and for his continued happiness.

Nor did I have any doubt that my prayers would be answered. For somehow I knew that everything had been worked out long ago by "the Lord, Saint Martin, and all of us."

Bridgeport, October 1993

"Holy and Wholesome"

It was to be my first funeral. I was home from the seminary in Rome for but a few weeks and just beginning to learn the duties of a curate at Holy Name Cathedral Parish in Chicago.

The announcement on the rectory bulletin board was quite clear: "Funeral Mass tomorrow morning at 10:30. Father Egan." Somewhat unnerved, I spent several hours that night reviewing the rubrics of the liturgy and preparing my sermon.

The following morning, robed in black vestments of the era and led by two servers in starched white surplices, I made my way to the altar, eyes cast down and chalice firmly in hand. Not until the Collect, or "Prayer" of the Mass, did I turn around to see the congregation.

It was two ladies and two gentlemen, all very much up in years, kneeling together in the front row. In the center aisle there stood a sturdy brass-colored trolley on which had been placed a simple wooden coffin covered in gray felt. At the rear of the cathedral, two young men were making a quiet visit, and above in the choir loft, the organist sat motionless.

The name of the deceased was typed on a card that the sacristan had placed on the altar. I took the card with me to the pulpit. Next to the name were the words: "Catholic Charities funeral. No known relatives or friends."

＞

That evening at supper, the senior curate, who had served at the cathedral with incredible dedication for almost twenty years, asked me how the funeral had gone. "We have three or four of those Catholic Charities funerals a week," he observed, "and the congregation is always pretty much the same."

"Did you meet Emily?" one of the younger curates inquired.

"Who is Emily?" I asked.

"She usually sits in the front row with a group of friends," I was told. "Every morning she checks with Lillian at the switchboard to find out if there is to be a Catholic Charities funeral the next day. Emily doesn't want anyone going to the Lord alone."

As it happened, the next week I was assigned to two other such funerals, and the congregation was always the same. They followed the coffin in. They prayed the funeral Mass devoutly. And they followed the coffin out. Anyone happening into the cathedral would have assumed that they were elderly relatives or friends of the deceased.

＞

It was several weeks later that I made the acquaintance of Emily and the other members of the funeral Mass congregation. I was passing a Mexican diner on Chicago Avenue one afternoon. The four of them were seated in a booth near the window. They waved and beckoned me to join them.

It was immediately clear which was Emily. She was said to be in her late seventies, but stood ramrod straight and spoke with a commanding voice. "We have been looking forward to meeting you, Father," she announced. "We have been seeing you at the funerals a good deal lately."

With that, she extracted from her large handbag about twenty pieces of notebook paper that were rolled up and clipped together at the top. She laid them out on the diner's table and reviewed the funeral Masses I had celebrated. This one was for Charles, and I had spoken of the mercy of God. This other one was for Cynthia, and I had spoken of the joy that would be ours in Heaven. This third one was for Gilberto, and I had spoken of the Lord's sacrificial death on the Cross for all without exception.

And so it went. I could hardly believe my eyes and ears. Each of the funerals was meticulously recorded on an individual sheet of paper at the top of which was written in Spencerian script words from the twelfth chapter of the second book of the Maccabees: "It is a holy and a wholesome thought to pray for the dead."

"A holy and a wholesome thought." Emily read the words slowly and with evident pleasure.

"But why do you do all of this?" I asked, immediately regretting that I had not formulated my question more diplomatically.

"The Communion of Saints," one of the elderly gentlemen replied without a moment's hesitation.

"Of course," Emily interjected, "the Communion of Saints. All of us in the Church—whether in Heaven, in Purgatory, or still here on earth—are one family under God, our Father, with Jesus, our Brother. We are the Communion of Saints, and if we are truly that, we have to take care of one another."

There was a moment of silence, but only a moment. Emily had much more to say.

"The dear departed that Catholic Charities send to Holy Name for the funerals," she explained, "are our brothers and sisters in the Lord, members of our Church, and members of our 'communion.' They deserve to have caring loved ones praying for them at their funeral Masses, and we do our best not to disappoint them. We treat them like relatives."

"Or at least like very close friends," the other lady added.

There was a second moment of silence, longer than the first. It was broken by the gentleman who had spoken earlier. "We do it," he stated as though replying to my original question for the first time, "because of the Communion of Saints."

Emily and the other nodded in total agreement.

❧

Not long after the conversation in the diner, I was transferred to live a few blocks away in the residence of the cardinal. All the same, I regularly made a visit to the Blessed Sacrament in the cathedral before going to lunch in the rectory dining room, where the cardinal and his immediate staff shared the noonday meal with the pastor and his curates.

Often I would witness the conclusion of a Catholic Charities funeral with the "saints" walking slowly behind a felt-covered coffin that bore another "saint" whom they had never met but loved and prayed for nonetheless. I knew that a new page had been inscribed with words from the second book of Maccabees, and I knew, too, that something altogether "holy and wholesome" had just taken place.

Bridgeport, January 1992

Humility Framed

Shortly before my tenth anniversary as bishop of Bridgeport, an elderly monsignor sent me an envelope containing several photographs of the prelate who had called me to the priesthood, Samuel Cardinal Stritch, the archbishop of Chicago.[5] The monsignor had been the cardinal's secretary for almost twenty years and knew of my esteem for his former "boss."

Inside the envelope was a note that read: "I hope you enjoy seeing these. They are yours to keep. I have others."

I looked through the collection with much interest and pleasure. In one of the photographs, the cardinal is standing on the steps of the chapel of the major seminary of the Archdiocese of Chicago with his chancellor and the seminary rector. In another he is celebrating Mass in his cathedral church. And in a third, my favorite, he is seated in one of the waiting rooms of the Vatican palace in full cardinalatial regalia, smiling and listening to a short, rotund clergyman who, perhaps because of the angle at which the photograph was taken, appears to be scolding him.

As I studied the third photograph, my mind raced back to April 1958.

[5] Samuel Cardinal Stritch served as Archbishop of Chicago from 1940 to 1958.

On a rainy spring day, I was seated in the backseat of a Fiat making its way home from Rome to Naples. Beside me was the rector of the seminary in Vatican City in which I was then completing my theological studies. He was a tall, austere bishop who had ordained me a priest just five months earlier. Seldom had I seen him display much emotion in the four years in which he had been my superior.

On this occasion, however, he was clearly both moved and upset. "They should never have insisted on bringing him here," he grumbled. "He's too old. He will not be able to adjust to life in Italy. It is a shame, a dreadful shame."

The person about whom he was speaking was Cardinal Stritch. Three months before our car trip to Naples, the cardinal had been appointed pro-prefect of the Sacred Congregation for the Propagation of the Faith by the Holy Father, Pope Pius XII. It was understood that, within a short time, the prefect of this Vatican office for the missions would step aside and Cardinal Stritch would be in charge.

Although the appointment was interpreted in some quarters as a sign of esteem, for Cardinal Stritch it was nothing of the sort. He was seventy years old. His health had always been delicate. And, most importantly, he seriously doubted that he was up to the challenge. Indeed, rumor had it that he had sent a friend, the archbishop of Detroit, to Rome to plead that the assignment be withdrawn.

Whatever of this, the assignment was not withdrawn. Thus, early in April, Cardinal Stritch and his priest-secretary boarded the S.S. *Constitution* in New York for the nine-day voyage to Naples.

On the fourth day out of port, however, a thrombosis developed in the cardinal's right arm. Radio dispatches were relayed first between New York and Naples and then between Chicago and Rome. It was agreed that there could be no turning back. The ship was to proceed to Italy at full speed.

❧

When the rector and I arrived at the bustling Neapolitan seaport, reporters and photographers were everywhere. The rector directed me to follow him up the gangplank but to stay in the corridor of the main deck while he, as the ranking American cleric in Rome, went to greet the cardinal in his cabin.

"If he is well enough to receive you, I will let you know," he announced rather solemnly. "Otherwise, you will have to wait to see him in Rome."

I took my place in the corridor, quietly reciting the Rosary. After two or three minutes, the rector appeared and gestured me to follow him down the gangplank. He said nothing until we were back in the car. "It doesn't look good," he reported, and he sank into silence.

Good it certainly was not. The cardinal was taken off the ship on a stretcher and hastened by ambulance to Rome, where a celebrated Italian surgeon amputated his arm at the shoulder. "The arm was dead," the surgeon informed the Roman newspaper *Il Messaggero*, rather inelegantly. "We were too late to save it."

❧

Three days after the operation, the monsignor who sent me the photographs telephoned to invite me and the three other seminary students from Chicago to the residence on the Via Sardegna where the cardinal was staying. We were to attend his Mass and join him for luncheon.

The Mass was unforgettable. The right sleeve of the cardinal's alb swung limply as he moved about the altar, but his voice was strong and he refused any assistance. When he raised the consecrated host in his left hand, his eyes fixed on it with incredible intensity, and he remained in that position far longer than was the custom of the time. An English priest in the back of the chapel strived unsuccessfully to muffle a sob.

The cardinal laid the consecrated host on the altar and, steadying himself with the only hand he had, genuflected in such a way that his forehead rested for perhaps a minute against the altar. Never had I witnessed a more moving or more beautiful posture of prayer.

The English priest sobbed a second time as the cardinal raised the chalice and then, with the most profound humility, once again sank to his knees in adoration.

⁀

At the lunch table, I was seated directly across from the cardinal as his "newest priest." He moved the pasta around his plate, sipped the wine, and insisted on talking about what the other seminarians and I were studying at the university. I tried to steer the conversation toward the extraordinary affection the faithful of Chicago had exhibited as their shepherd departed, but he did not pick up on the subject.

I next inquired as delicately as I could about the dramatic events during his ocean crossing. Again, he gently dismissed the issue and returned to the matter of our studies.

"The Fathers of the Church," he proclaimed, "you must read them and meditate them if you wish to gain an authentic understanding of the Scriptures. It is the Fathers who open up the true meaning of Holy Writ. Without them there is no telling into what misinterpretations and misconceptions one might fall."

It all seemed unreal. Here was a man who had just lost his arm, and he was concerned only with us and our theological studies.

Interpreting the worried looks of the six priests who had attended the Mass and were with us for the luncheon, I twice suggested that we leave so that the cardinal might rest. Twice he told me that he wanted to be with "my new priest and my seminarists" and proceeded to launch into another set of observations about the Fathers of the Church. We settled into our chairs and listened in wonder and admiration.

～

Two days later, the seminary rector called me to his office. He had just received a telephone call from the cardinal's secretary. His Eminence had passed away.

I told the rector about the Mass and the luncheon, describing the genuflections and repeating the theological admonitions almost verbatim.

He turned in his swivel chair to gaze out the window at the children's hospital next to the seminary.

"Keep this week ever alive in your memory," he whispered. "At the Mass and luncheon with the cardinal you were taught a powerful lesson in humility, obedience, and selflessness. You witnessed up close the love and concern for his future priests on the part of an aging bishop who was undoubtedly in considerable pain. Yet, never forget any of this.

"Think about it often, and treasure it always," the rector concluded. "It will serve you well in your service to the Lord and His holy people."

Practice for Heaven

He did not look at me but signaled that I was free to leave. I suspect that there were tears in his eyes that he did not want me to see. Certainly there were tears in mine, which I was too anxious to keep to myself. They were those kind of tears.

⁓

The department store Caldor was having a sale. I pulled into the parking lot of the one on Hawley Lane in Trumbull. Under my arm was an envelope containing a photograph.

I went immediately to the department in the far corner of the store where picture frames are displayed and found one that fit the photograph quite well. A sign above it declared that it had been reduced by 30 percent.

It now sits atop a file case in the little room that I use as an office in my home, where any time I wish I can study the image and recall the goodness of a kind and self-effacing prelate who appears to be receiving a scolding with a marvelously humble smile.

Bridgeport, March 1999

Stations

The senior judge of the Vatican's highest judicial tribunal, the Sacred Roman Rota, was greatly concerned. One of our fellow judges, a Scot, who was a dear friend of mine, was in a hospital in London with a brain tumor. The senior judge felt that I should go to see him and assure him of the prayers and best wishes of all at the Rota.

It was April, and I was only too willing to accept the assignment. Thus, reservations were quickly made at a hotel in Russell Square, a short distance from the hospital where my colleague was confined, and I was on my way.

⁓

London can, of course, be cold and rainy, but this April it was marvelously warm and sunny. Never had I found the city more inviting.

I arrived at Heathrow Airport late in the morning, checked into my hotel around two, and hurried over to the hospital for the afternoon visiting hours. My friend was in a ward. His head had been shaved for an operation that was scheduled for the next day, and he wore a kind of nightcap about which the two of us did much joking. I brought him the greetings of the judges and staff of the Rota, and we chatted until a rather severe nurse invited me to leave.

The next day was as splendid as the day before. Early in the morning, I took a long walk, ending up at a small Catholic church in a quiet residential neighborhood. The heavy front doors stood wide open, as did the glass doors that led from the vestibule into the nave of the church. On either side of the vestibule were small wooden benches fitted with velvet cushions. I went in, and as I moved up the aisle, a tall man in a smock that reached well below his knees approached to introduce himself as the sexton of the church.

Did I wish to celebrate Mass? he inquired. I replied that I did. Accordingly, he directed me to a tiny sacristy, laid out a set of vestments, and served at the altar with the air of a seasoned professional.

⁀

After Mass, I went to the aisle seat in the last pew on the left, knelt for a brief prayer of thanksgiving, and then sat to recite the Office of the day. The sun pierced through the stained-glass windows. The church was silent, and my prayers were for the judge in the nearby hospital.

As I was about to conclude the section of the Office that is known as Matins, I heard a good deal of noise first on the porch of the church and then in the vestibule. An elderly gentleman in an overcoat that seemed a bit much for a warm spring day entered, leaning heavily on two metal canes. Though there was no one in the church apart from myself, he motioned me to move further into my pew and sank into the aisle seat with a thump.

"I always sit here," he reported. "No handles."

At first, I did not understand. Soon, however, I realized that all of the pews except this one had brass fittings on the armrest close to the aisle, fittings that would render a disabled person's entry somewhat precarious. I smiled and returned to my Office.

After a few minutes, the man extracted from his coat a rather tattered pamphlet, fixed his eyes intently on something in the front of the church, and began to recite from the pamphlet under his breath. "We adore Thee, O Christ, and we bless Thee, because by Thy Holy Cross Thou hast redeemed the world," he whispered.

Line by line, he read the familiar meditations of Saint Alphonsus Liguori on the Stations of the Cross, and before each new Station, he again fixed his eyes on something ahead.

I pretended not to notice what was happening. All the same, after the Third Station my pew companion evidently decided that an explanation was in order.

"I cannot walk very well anymore," he observed, "but I make the Stations of the Cross as best I can. I look hard at each Station on the wall, I recite the prayers sitting here, and I ask the crucified Savior to do the walking for me."

He paused a moment and added in a voice that I could scarcely hear, "He walked the Stations for all of us the first time, Father. I'm sure He doesn't mind doing it again for me."

I was so touched by his words that I closed my Breviary and pondered them with genuine delight, even after the man had stumbled out of the pew and out of the church as well.

Inspired and uplifted, I returned to the hospital. My colleague from Rome had been informed that his operation was being postponed. He did not know why, but neither did he seem concerned. We chatted for about a half hour until another nurse brought our conversation to an end.

I walked out into the sun. The British Museum was just a few blocks away. It had been my plan to go there and spend the remainder of the morning admiring the Magna Carta, the Gutenberg Bible, the Elgin Marbles, and such. Something, however, brought me back to the church where I had celebrated Mass.

This time, too, the heavy front doors were open, although the glass doors of the vestibule were closed and locked. I sat on one of the benches in the vestibule and, looking through the glass doors, peered into the church. Thanks to a particularly bright sun, I could see the outlines of most of the Stations.

Thus, moved by some unknown grace, I began to pray, "We adore Thee, O Christ, and we bless Thee," and sitting there, first on the left and then on the right, I traveled with my eyes from Station to Station, reciting all that I could remember from the meditations of Saint Alphonsus and trusting that the Lord would be willing to do the walking for me, too.

⁓

Early the next morning, I returned to the hospital to inquire about the time of my friend's operation so that I might make a report by telephone to the senior judge of the Sacred Roman Rota. The news was not at all what I had expected. Two of my friend's physicians saw me in a visiting room and announced that there was no hope for their patient. "The tumor is simply too large," one of them explained.

My spirits were exceedingly low. Thus, I returned to the church where I had been celebrating morning Mass. It was noontime, and both sets of doors stood wide open.

Stations

I entered and found myself alone except for one other, the Redeemer Who had walked the Stations for me the day before. I told Him of my hurt. I commended my friend to His loving care. And the two of us walked the Stations again — this time together.

New York, March 2007

No Telescoping

She was a nurse working in an upscale hospital on the Near-North Side of Chicago. The afternoon she came to see me at the rectory of Chicago's Holy Name Cathedral she was in a white uniform with a coat thrown over her shoulders. From her manner and tone of voice, it was clear that she was not at all happy about the visit.

"I am going to be married in a Catholic church in Michigan," she announced. "My fiancé is Catholic, I am not, and I understand that the Catholic Church requires me to have six lessons on Catholic teachings about marriage before we can have the wedding. Where does one take these lessons?"

"I will be happy to give them to you whenever you like," I replied. "Have you any times in mind?"

"My fiancé is coming to Chicago next week," she answered. "Give me your telephone number. We will call you for the necessary appointments."

I handed her the number on a sheet of rectory stationery. She took it, turned on her heel, and strode out the door without so much as a good-bye.

The following week, she telephoned to say that she would like to see me that evening. I told her that I was free and looked forward to our getting together again.

At the appointed hour, she appeared with her fiancé following unenthusiastically behind.

"He is here," she observed with a meaningful, not to say menacing, edge to her voice, "because I don't want him to miss even a word."

I forced a smile, and the three of us sat down around my desk, on which were several copies of a little blue handbook entitled *Six Lessons in Preparation for a Mixed Marriage*. I gave one to each of my guests.

"When there is sufficient cause, such as when one or both parties are living at a distance," I noted, "Church law permits us to telescope the six lessons into three. Perhaps under the circumstances we could ..."

The nurse interrupted immediately. "No telescoping!" she cried. "I don't want him to miss even a word."

The fiancé kept his eyes fixed nervously on the ceiling. We agreed on five more appointments, and I launched into the first lesson.

⟾

Lesson 1 had to do with the history of matrimony. I recounted the story of Adam in the Garden of Eden and the Lord's desire that he not be alone. I told of marriage in the Old Testament, emphasizing examples of virtuous married life, especially in the books of Tobias and Ruth. And I completed my presentation with a commentary on the most important statements of the Lord and Saint Paul on the dignity of marriage and the duties of husbands and wives.

The nurse seemed a bit less antagonistic as she and her fiancé were putting on their coats to leave.

"I knew all of that, sir," she remarked. "But it was interesting to hear how you would say it."

Lesson 2 concerned the nature of matrimony as a fundamental human institution. I explained that the marriage bond is forged when a man and a woman agree to give to and receive from each other an altogether unique right — the perpetual and exclusive right to acts that normally and by their very nature lead to the procreation of children, acts whereby husband and wife can become co-creators with their God.

"Co-creators!" the nurse exclaimed. "I have never heard that before. What a lovely idea! Co-creators with their God. Why, that's lovely. Simply stunning."

The fiancé reported that he also found it agreeable.

"One of the Brothers in my high school used to say that," he recalled. "He always told us that basically this is what makes marriage so wonderful and . . ." He hesitated for a moment. "And so holy, too."

The nurse shook my hand and smiled as she and her fiancé were leaving. The fiancé looked somewhat relaxed for the first time.

⁀

Lessons 3 and 4 were on the indissolubility of the marriage bond and the fidelity required of the married couple. Some of the nurse's original antipathy returned during my defense of indissolubility. She reminded me that "many good Christian people" approve of divorce and that, as far as she knew, serious opposition to it was coming almost exclusively from "the Roman Church."

I reviewed all the relevant citations from Scripture to no avail. The nurse was sure that somehow they could not mean what they seemed to say. I was about to take another tack when the fiancé took her by the hand and looked squarely into her eyes.

"Sweetheart," he said almost in a whisper, "who gets hurt by divorce?"

She did not answer.

"Well, I'll tell you," he went on. "Who gets hurt first and foremost are the wife and the children, the ones who are most vulnerable and most in need of being cared for and protected. You know that. We both know it. And that's why the good God made it that a marriage is to last—forever."

I was not sure how a professional theologian would react to this approach, but I watched it achieve its effect with remarkable speed.

"That's right," the nurse proclaimed almost indignantly. "Of course, that's right." She was silent for a moment and then turned to me. "My fiancé," she declared, "is a wonderful, good man."

When we were together for the next session on fidelity, twice she reminded me of these qualities in her future husband, and with each reminder he smiled broadly. By the end of the lesson they have moved their chairs closer together, and they sat across the desk from me, hand in hand.

~

The fifth lesson focused on chastity in marriage. Here, too, I had expected a challenge at least about the matter of openness to children, but none was forthcoming. The couple had evidently read the relevant chapter in their handbooks and agreed on its message.

It was the final lesson, however, the one on matrimony as a sacrament, that evoked the most emotional response. I read the passage from chapter 5 of the epistle of Saint Paul to the Ephesians, where marriage is described as an image of the loving union of the Savior with His Church.

"Here is, above all else, what makes the marriage of the baptized sacred," I asserted. "It is a sign or, as we say, a sacrament, that shows forth the relationship of limitless devotion between God's Son and God's People. What could be more beautiful? What could be more powerful? What could be more inspiring for a man and a woman preparing to be married?"

The nurse responded in a voice so low that I could hardly hear it. "Nothing, Father," she said. "Nothing." This was the first time she had addressed me as "Father." I rose from my chair and simply announced that our lessons were over.

⁓

A month or so later, I met the nurse in the hospital while visiting an ailing parishioner. She told me that she had decided to become a Catholic and was enrolled in an inquiry class at the parish near her apartment.

"What you taught us about Church teaching covering matrimony did the trick," she announced. "Please, Father, never 'telescope' any of it."

Bridgeport, January 1995

Very Special Prayers

When I first met him, he was seventy-five years of age and retired. I had arrived in Rome in December 1972 to begin my new duties as a judge on the Tribunal of the Sacred Roman Rota. The day after my arrival, he telephoned to ask if he might come to see me. I was both delighted and flattered.

His name was famous among canon lawyers across the world. Before being named a judge of the Rota in 1948, he had been a celebrated professor at a law school in the Midwest. While serving on the Rota, he had authored a dozen of more books on legal ethics, tribunal procedure, and marriage law as well as scores of judicial decisions that were quoted far and wide.

After retiring, he had continued to live in the Eternal City, where, in the judgment of many, he was the most Roman of the Romans. He arrived at my apartment at five-thirty in the evening, the Roman visiting hour. He was wearing a black cassock, a black tasseled sash, and a broad-rimmed Roman hat. In a few minutes, I felt as though I had known him all my life.

"*Salve, Reverendissime Pater,*" he intoned in Latin with a chuckle and an embrace. "I welcome you, and I assure you that I am eager to be of help in any way I can."

With that he sat down on the sofa in my study and opened a huge briefcase from which he extracted about a hundred typewritten pages containing what he described as "all you need to know, as far as procedure is concerned, to get a case started properly and to bring it to a wise and brisk conclusion."

The pages having been consigned to a table next to the sofa, he then produced a shopping bag and drew out of it three packages that he had evidently wrapped himself. He beamed as I opened each. The first contained a pair of carpet-slippers; the second, a fountain pen; and the third, a two-volume Latin-Italian dictionary.

"Now," he inquired, settling back into the sofa, "how do you feel about your new assignment, and how can I give you a hand?"

The conversation lasted almost two hours. When my guest left, I could hardly believe how relaxed and encouraged I felt. He had given me his private telephone number. He had offered to lend me any of his books that I might need. He had even promised to remember me by name each and every day at Mass.

~

As the years passed, the visits continued. On several occasions, I asked if I might not come to his residence, thus sparing him the trip through Roman traffic. He always said no and finally one evening explained why.

"I have a list of people whom I visit regularly," he announced. "Some are ill. Some are alone. Some may one day need my help or counsel. All are my very special flock, and my visits to them are my very special prayers."

He paused for a moment and then went on. "Before I leave my apartment, I make the Sign of the Cross and beg the Lord to lend me His lips and, especially, His ears during my visit. And when I get back home, I conclude my prayer with another Sign of the Cross."

He paused again. "You wouldn't want to deprive an old man of his very special prayers, would you?" he asked with a broad smile. "I never had the privilege of being a pastor who could visit his people week after week, year after year. So now I have put together my own parish with a rather impressive roster of parishioners."

I accompanied him to his car, returned to my apartment, and found on the floor next to where he had been sitting a package on which he had written my name. Evidently he had intended to give it to me but forgot in the course of the explanation of his visits.

The package contained four books, all translations of works on the spiritual life which, I learned from the prefaces, he had "revised, adapted, and modernized," and paid to have printed "for private distribution." I telephoned to inquire about the books.

"Oh, I am glad you found them," he said. "They are my other very special prayers. I will tell you about them the next time we get together."

⁀⁾

The next time came very soon. Indeed, within a week he telephoned to ask to come to see me and arrived with another package of books under his arm.

"I usually do not tell people about my very special prayers," he declared as he sipped an espresso I had prepared for him. "But, since you know about the visits, you might just as well know about the books, too."

He adjusted himself in his chair and continued. "Every day, for four or five hours, I translate or revise the translation of spiritual books that are either not in English or not in very good English. I send them to friends in the United States and Great

Britain whom I cannot visit the way I visit you. That makes my parish even bigger than Rome."

He motioned for another espresso without interrupting his discourse. "Each day, before I begin my translating or revising, I make the Sign of the Cross and beg the Lord for wisdom and patience; and when I finish, I make the Sign of the Cross again, and my prayer is over. So now you know about all of my very special prayers."

In my library today are seventeen spiritual books received from my guest during his visits. They range from well-known masterpieces by Saint Teresa of Ávila, Saint Francis de Sales, and Abbot Joseph Marmion, to lesser-known works by Saint Jane Frances de Chantal, Abbot Vital Lehodey, and John Eusebius Nieremberg, S.J. All of them are treasured for what they are: very special prayers received on the occasion of very special prayers.

꙰

Toward the end of April in 1982, my guest's housekeeper telephoned to ask me to come to see him. I found him in bed with a high fever and little strength. He was admitted to a Blue Sisters' hospital the following day. A week later, as I stood next to his bed reciting the Memorare of Saint Bernard of Clairvaux, he went to His Lord quietly and with the hint of a smile on his face.

The nurse in attendance asked if I were the next of kin.

Fighting back tears, I replied, "No, just one of his parishioners."

Bridgeport, June 1993

Profession

The evening meal was over. It was the winter of 1956. Three hundred strong, we seminarians filed out of the dining room of the Pontifical North American College, which prepares young men to serve as priests in dioceses and archdioceses throughout the United States. A faculty member was stationed at the end of the corridor. He beckoned to me.

"The rector is in his room," he said. "He would like to speak with you."

I made my way up to the fifth-floor living-quarters of Bishop Martin J. O'Connor, the seminary rector since 1946. He had been an auxiliary bishop of the Diocese of Scranton and had been the pastor of a parish in Wilkes-Barre, Pennsylvania, when he was named to the rectorship of the college in his late forties.

Arriving in Rome, he found that the seminary building near the Trevi Fountain had been taken over by the Italian government and turned into an orphanage. He won it back in court and restored it. He also reclaimed and refurbished the summer residence of the college in Castel Gandolfo outside Rome and, in 1952, saw to the completion of a magnificent new seminary building on the Janiculum Hill, a short distance from the Vatican.

In later years, while remaining rector, he became the first president of the Pontifical Commission for Social Communications;

virtually the author of *Inter Mirifica*, the first document issued by the Second Vatican Council; the papal nuncio to Malta; a titular archbishop; and much more. He was an impressive figure, and we seminarians, whether we admitted it or not, were all quite impressed.

⁀

I knocked at the door. A voice from within responded with the familiar Italian "*Avanti.*"

I entered and found the rector emerging from a small private chapel attached to the living room of his apartment. The candles on the altar were lit, and the door of the tabernacle stood open, revealing a ciborium inside.

He motioned to me to be seated on a chair across from his just outside the chapel.

"Tomorrow morning," he began in the low, solemn voice we seminarians loved to imitate, "I will celebrate the Mass and preside at the profession of a religious Sister. She was not well when her class was professed. This is a special ceremony just for her."

He sat silent for a moment and then went on. "The organist of the motherhouse will not be available. Hence, I would like you to come with me and the student master of ceremonies. It will be enough if you just play an accompaniment for the Gregorian Mass of Angels on the organ. We will be leaving from the front door at 5:30."

I assured the rector that I would be at the front door at the stipulated hour and, perhaps a bit boldly, inquired about the candles that were lit on the chapel altar and the open tabernacle door.

"I am preparing for tomorrow morning," he explained. "The preparation will continue until the ceremony begins. There will be a holy hour in the presence of the Blessed Sacrament this evening, a meditation on the evangelical counsels of poverty, chastity, and obedience after I rise in the morning, and prayerful recollection until we go to the altar for Mass. This is the program, Edward, and you should understand the reason for it."

Again, he was silent for a moment as though to collect his thoughts.

"Tomorrow," he said, "I am being granted the grace of witnessing the giving of an entire life to Christ and His Church. A religious is freely choosing the Lord above all else without condition or reservation. And the Lord, in His gracious providence, is allowing me to represent His Mystical Body on this marvelously holy occasion. For this, I need prayer and recollection — first and foremost, prayer and recollection."

The repeating of words and phrases was another characteristic of the rector's manner of speaking that we, his seminarians, mimicked with much pleasure. It was his way of emphasizing key points, and it usually signaled that a conference or interview had drawn to a close.

An elderly layman who had worked for the seminary even before the war drove us through the dark, narrow streets of the Eternal City with the casual disdain for stop signs and traffic lights that makes motoring in Rome never less than an adventure. Yet the often wary rector did not seem to notice as he led the student master of ceremonies, the driver, and me in reciting the Rosary in Italian. This was evidently part of the "prayer and recollection" about which he had spoken the night before.

Not a word was exchanged among the four of us. Recollected, we sat motionless; and quietly, we prayed.

At the motherhouse, I learned that the regular organist had appeared and that there was accordingly no need of me. The student master of ceremonies suggested that I assist him at the altar.

"You can take the rector's ring when he washes his hands," he said with a wry smile.

The liturgy was for me deeply moving, even though my part in it was little more than what the student master of ceremonies had indicated. At the washing of hands before the Mass, toward the end of the Offertory and after Communion, I dutifully took the rector's episcopal ring and, when he had finished drying his hands, returned it to him. It was a rather ornate piece of ecclesiastical jewelry, with a chalice engraved on one side of the setting, a bishop's miter engraved on the other, and a large green malachite stone fitted into the center.

The rector's sermon was brief, and the theme came as no surprise to me. It was an elaboration of what he had told me the night before about religious profession and the reverence that was owed to it.

⁓

On January 1, 1991, Sister Marie Dolores Ballotta of the Sisters Minor of Mary Immaculate, a new religious congregation for the Diocese of Bridgeport, made her solemn profession in the splendidly renovated church of Holy Name of Jesus Parish in Stamford, Connecticut. The mother general and foundress of the Congregation had come from Rome for the ceremony, which was attended by hundreds of Holy Name of Jesus parishioners.

The Mass, which I had the privilege of celebrating, and the profession, at which I presided, were for me especially inspiring. When Sister Mary Dolores came before the mother general to recite her vows, words from the distant past rushed into my mind:

Profession

"I am being granted the grace of officially witnessing the giving of an entire life to Christ and His Church. A religious is freely choosing the Lord above all else without condition or reservation, and the Lord is allowing me to represent His Mystical Body on this marvelously holy occasion."

I whispered a prayer of thanksgiving that, recalling the example of my seminary rector, I had made a holy hour in the presence of the Blessed Sacrament the night before, meditated on the evangelical counsels of poverty, chastity, and obedience after I rose in the morning, and even recited the Rosary with the diocesan master of ceremonies as we drove from Stratford, where I lived, to Stamford.

⁀

There was, however, one small snag in the ceremony. The episcopal ring I was wearing was too large and kept slipping up and down my finger. It was a rather ornate piece of ecclesiastical jewelry with a chalice engraved on one side of the setting, a bishop's miter engraved on the other, and a large green malachite stone fitted into the center.

It had been left to me in his will by an archbishop who had passed away in Wilkes-Barre in 1986; an archbishop who had ordained me to the priesthood, on whose seminary faculty I had served as a young priest, and from whom as a seminarian I had learned with splendid power and clarity the beauty and wonder of religious profession.

Bridgeport, February 1993

Beyond the Sea

"Was Jesus Christ truly the Son of God?" we were asked. "Why did His Father in Heaven not wait until Jesus Christ was an old man before He had to die on the Cross?" "Did someone take care of His mother after Jesus Christ went to Heaven?" "Do all except Chinese people know about Jesus Christ?" "Why is there no mention of Jesus Christ on BBC discs?" "Do all followers of Jesus Christ love God with all their hearts and their neighbor as themselves?" "Will someone be coming sometime to Nanning to tell us about Jesus Christ?"

Chapters

It was almost too small even to be called a hotel, for it boasted only thirty-two rooms, a tiny lobby, and a slightly larger breakfast area on the top floor. Still, because it was marvelously clean and located in the center of Paris, a few blocks from the Place de la Concorde, I considered it just about ideal.

A week before Christmas in 1957, my parents and I, reservations in hand, arrived as guests. On December 15, I had been ordained a priest in Rome, and we were taking advantage of the "Christmas break" to explore some of France and Switzerland together after four years of my being away from home.

Each morning we would meet in the hotel lobby to go to Mass in one of the nearby churches. This practice soon caught the attention of the director of the hotel and his wife, both of whom, after the first day, joined us each morning for breakfast when we returned from Mass. Before long they were becoming fast friends with my father and especially with my mother, who spoke French quite well.

"You American Catholics put us to shame," the hotel director announced one morning. "We French have had the Faith so long that we no longer treasure it as we should. We need to start learning from you."

At least a small measure of such "learning" ensued on the last morning of our stay in Paris, when the hotel director and his wife went with us to Mass at the nearby Church of the Madeleine. At breakfast afterward, the director's wife presented my mother with a *gâteau au chocolat* to take with us to England, where my parents would in a few days be boarding a ship for New York. We would enjoy the cake particularly in London, the director's wife confided, because the cuisine in that city "leaves much to be desired."

⤳

Six years later almost to the day, I checked into the same hotel. I was in Paris again during a Christmas break to work on my doctoral dissertation in the National Library of France.

The director of the hotel and his wife recognized me immediately. Before giving me the key to my room, they brought me up to the breakfast area, sat me down, and questioned me at length about my parents. Some years before, they reported, my mother had sent them a Christmas card, and they were "ever so grateful."

"Will you be joining me for Mass?" I asked perhaps a bit too quickly.

"Probably not," the director responded, his face darkening. "We are rather short-handed at this time, and well, we can talk about that later."

⤳

Two days passed. I went to Mass alone and ate my breakfast alone. The director and his wife were nowhere to be seen. A young waiter brought me and the other guests our coffee and croissants.

On the third evening, I came back to the hotel quite late from a piano recital at the Salle Pleyel around the corner on the Rue du Faubourg Saint-Honoré. The director and his wife were in the lobby behind the small reservations desk. Snow was falling outside, and I was both cold and wet.

"Come upstairs for coffee," the director called from across the lobby. "You need something to warm you up."

Seated in the breakfast area, I set the program of the piano recital on the table. It was just a listing of the works to be performed without program notes.

"Did you enjoy the recital?" the director inquired.

"Not particularly," I replied. "Most of the music was unfamiliar to me."

He picked up the program and examined it. "But certainly not the suite by Ravel," he exclaimed. "Certainly you are familiar with the *Gaspard de la Nuit* of Maurice Ravel."

"Frankly, I am not," I confessed. "I have heard of it, but that is about all. And I cannot say that I found it terribly interesting."

"What a pity!" the director shot back. "Father, it is a delight. It is a masterpiece."

⁊

The next morning, as I was leaving for Mass, I found a book leaning against the door of my hotel room. Its worn, cardboard cover clearly revealed that it had been read and reread by its owner and perhaps by others as well.

Inside, on the title page, the director of the hotel had written a dedication: "A gift for my priest friend. Please read chapter 7. Then trust Ravel's genius and give *Gaspard de la Nuit* another hearing. I am sure you will come to love it, as I do." The chapter in question was entitled "Appreciating Ravel's Suites for the Piano."

In the lobby I met the wife of the director and tried to express my gratitude for the book. She, however, interrupted me nervously and spoke quickly. She was sorry that they had not gone to Mass with me, but, as her husband had intended to explain, he was no longer "inspired" by the Mass. She hoped that I understood.

～

I was to leave that day. Thus, after breakfast I hurried to one of the gigantic department stores on the Boulevard Haussmann to purchase perfume for my mother and sister. On my way to the cashier, I was surprised to see a small religious-goods section in the next aisle. I went over to it and began to rummage through its modest collection of spiritual books. One was *An Introduction to the Devout Life* by Saint Francis de Sales, a classic that I had read several times. I paid for it and the perfume and fairly ran back to the hotel.

In my room I sat down at a tiny desk and wrote a dedication on the title page of the book I had purchased. It read: "A gift for my friend. Please read chapter 14 of part 2. Then trust in the genius of the Lord and give the Mass another hearing. I am sure that you will come to love it — again." The chapter in question was entitled, "Holy Mass and How One is to Participate in It."

Downstairs in the lobby, I paid the director for my stay and presented him with my gift. He read the title page, turned to the indicated chapter, read its title, and came out from behind the reservations desk to shake my hand.

"It's a deal," he proclaimed. "You read my chapter, and I'll read yours."

"Will you let me know the results?" I asked.

"No," he answered with a crooked smile. "That's between the Lord and me."

Back in Rome a few days later, I fulfilled my part of the bargain, though not perhaps as the director of the hotel might have imagined I would.

Kneeling in Saint Peter's Basilica under an imposing statue of Saint Francis de Sales high over my head, I read every word of "Appreciating the Piano Suites of Maurice Ravel," fully trusting that the saintly author of a chapter entitled "Holy Mass and How One Is to Participate in It" would take it from there.

Bridgeport, March 1992

El Perdón

Guidebook in hand, I made my way with a priest friend into the splendid Church of La Merced (Our Lady of Mercy) in Lima, Peru. It was a bright July morning in 1984. We had just left a nearby religious-goods store in which I had purchased a book about the sacrament of Penance, entitled *El Perdón* (Forgiveness). I slipped the book into a little canvas bag from the Peruvian airline, which contained as well a 35-millimeter camera that I greatly prized.

As I was leaving the church, after my priest friend had returned to our hotel for something he had forgotten, a woman of about sixty years of age approached me, gesticulating dramatically. The back of my jacket, she cried, was covered with a strange, green substance. Raising my arm, I saw that she was right.

Accordingly, I began to remove the jacket. In a flash the woman seized the airline bag and ran toward the door of the church. As I attempted to follow her, four young men with menacing eyes moved to block my path. It seemed the better part of valor to end the pursuit.

～

All the way back to my hotel, I grumbled to myself about what had befallen me. I lamented the loss of my camera. I imagined what I would do to the thief and her accomplices if I could ever get my hands on them. I even debated with myself about the punishment they deserved, and with each step the punishment grew more severe.

As I entered the rather tattered hotel lobby with the soiled jacket over my arm, the manager rushed over to greet me. It was clear that he had seen many other guests in a similar predicament.

"I am so sorry," he cried. "Please, come into my office. Sit down. We will have a cup of coffee together."

In the office, I briefly recounted what had transpired in the Church of La Merced. He listened patiently and then, with a tremor in his voice, launched into a monologue that I was sure he had recited many times before.

"We are not a criminal people," he began. "But we are hungry and hurting. Our young men cannot find work. Hundreds of peasants who can neither read nor write are flooding into Lima every day, and the resources of the city are long since stretched beyond any reasonable measure. We do not know where to turn. And some in their misery are reduced to doing the kind of thing that was done to you.

"But please understand," he continued. "We do not want to live this way. The vast majority of our people are decent and God-fearing. They want to earn their daily bread. They yearn to have families and care for them. But nothing is going their way. Nothing is getting better, or even promises to get better. Nothing. Nothing."

He finished his coffee and looked at me with world-weary eyes.

"I have had three wallets, two briefcases, and one wristwatch stolen from me in the streets of Lima," he said. "At first, I would get angry, make threats, conjure up in my mind what I would do to the thieves, and all of that. Now I go to my parish church and light a candle for those who have stolen from me. I tell the Lord that I have forgiven them, and I ask Him to forgive them as well. This does not bring back what I have lost. Still, it brings me closer to the Savior Who died on Calvary's hill for me, imploring His Father in Heaven to forgive those who were murdering Him. To me this is worth all the wallets, briefcases, and watches in the world."

With that, he rose and gently took my jacket from me, observing that the hotel would have it dry-cleaned and ready before my priest friend and I checked out.

⌒

That afternoon I passed the religious-goods store again and went in. I asked the lady behind the counter if she had another copy of *El Perdón*. She said she did and wrapped it up for me.

The next morning, as I was packing to leave, a knock came at the door. It was the hotel manager. In his hands he held my jacket professionally dry-cleaned with his business card attached and signed. He shook my hand, smiled, embraced me, and left.

I placed the jacket in my suitcase next to *El Perdón*. Now I had two treatises on forgiveness to bring home with me. I dared to hope that the printed one would prove to be as powerful as the one that was dry-cleaned.

Bridgeport, June 1990

The Return

The plane took off on time from Boston's Logan Airport. It was nine o'clock in the morning on Friday, January 23. We would be landing in Havana, Cuba, in less than four hours.

As I settled in for the journey, my mind sped back to 1965. I had just returned home after several years of teaching in Rome to be assigned to work in the chancery of the Archdiocese of Chicago.

The chancellor was a rather quiet man with little taste for casual conversation. "You know Italian and French," he said to me one morning as we mounted the steps of the chancery together. "Working with Spanish-speaking people should be no problem for you."

I tried to challenge the assumption, but my interlocutor continued without missing a beat. "There is a rather large community of exiled Cubans living in apartments near the North Side of the city," he reported. "I want you to arrange to celebrate Mass for them. My secretary will have the names and addresses of the couples who contacted me about their needs."

We entered the office, and he made his way up the old staircase that led to the second floor. Before reaching the top, he turned and added, "Let me know how this works out. These are a noble people, Father, noble people. Help them however you can."

⤳

In 1965, part of the Mass was in Latin and part in the vernacular. I had no problem with the former, but with the latter in Spanish there were some considerable difficulties. Hence, after two or three weeks of Sunday Masses for eighty to ninety Cubans in a large parish hall, I was invited to come the following Saturday to the apartment of one of the couples who had contacted the chancellor so that I might be provided with "some pointers about Spanish pronunciation."

The apartment was small and filled with members of the Cuban congregation. Shortly after my arrival, the lessons began, the principal teacher being a lady well into her sixties who confided that she had taught Spanish literature at the university level for over thirty years.

I was handed a book of sermonettes published in Cuba in the 1930s or 1940s and asked to begin reading the first of them aloud. Standing at the end of the dining room table, I launched into my recitation like a zealous schoolboy. The interruptions and corrections were frequent, but always kind and patient. Before long the lessons became a game, and soon I found myself eager to attend the Saturday-afternoon gatherings whenever I was free.

⤳

At the conclusion of my readings of the appointed sermonettes, coffee and cake would be served along with tiny glasses of rum, and a lively conversation never failed to ensue. Over and again, I was told of the beauties of Cuba, the cultural life of Havana, the *ajiaco criollo* (meat and vegetable soup), and an incredible variety of other culinary delights. The interiors of the churches were described in lavish detail. The so-called Eastern Beaches were depicted as the best in the world. I felt that I could almost touch the hurt and yearning for home that swirled about the room.

"One day we will all return," the oldest of the men loved to announce, and his wife regularly sighed and called his happy forecast into doubt.

"None of us, not even one, will ever make it back," she would lament. And with that she would tell me in almost always the same words of the haberdasher's shop she and her husband had maintained in Havana's Hotel Inglaterra, which she identified as "the grandest hotel in all of the city."

Her eyes would flash. "It was lovely," she would say. "Two splendid lobbies, many elegant guests, delightful music in the afternoon. Oh, how we miss it!"

⌒

My reverie ended as we were ordered to fasten our seatbelts for landing. We stared out the windows at the sprawling city below. From that point on, there would be no more daydreaming.

A bus carried us from the airport to our hotel. Along the way there were banners on every block welcoming "Juan Pablo II" and vaunting "Cuba Libre" (Free Cuba).

"This is the only road that has been repaired in years," the bus driver confided. "The government wanted it to be in good condition for the Pope."

We deposited our luggage in the hotel and were bused to a nearby convent for Mass. The brief journey left us all with every visitor's overriding impression of Cuba today: physically, it is crumbling—except for a handful of tourist hotels, virtually every building has lost part of its façade; nothing seems to have been painted in decades; and the streets are masses of potholes, strewn with brick and plaster debris.

At four o'clock the next morning, a group of us gathered in the hotel lobby ready to fly to Santiago de Cuba in the south-eastern corner of the island for Mass with the Holy Father. Our plane was a forty-five-year-old Russian aircraft whose propellers struggled mightily to keep us aloft.

In the huge park where we came together for Mass, excitement reigned. Tens of thousands applauded as we processed to the main altar. The heat was intense, but somehow Cubans and visitors alike adjusted to it as the Bishop of Rome took his place on a presider's chair that had been originally fashioned for Saint Anthony Mary Claret, founder of the Claretians and archbishop of Santiago de Cuba in the 1850s.

John Paul II was formally welcomed by the current arch-bishop of Santiago de Cuba, a much-admired shepherd of souls who had spent years in Cuban prisons. The archbishop's ad-dress was larded with incredibly pointed sound-bites. "Do not mistake 'El Partido' [the Communist Party] for 'La Nación' [The Nation]," he said. And again: "Do not think of 'El Pater-nalismo' [shorthand for the Castro regime] as 'El Patriotismo' [patriotism]." Many in the crowd gasped at his courage, while the brother of *Comandante* Castro sat in his place, rigid and unsmiling.

The Successor of Saint Peter began his homily with words from Psalm 32: "Blessed is the nation whose God is the Lord." He described the Church as a source of "peace and reconcilia-tion" which seeks nothing from government but the "freedom and dignity of all." Cheers were interlaced with sobs, as the seventy-seven-year-old Pontiff concluded with a prayer to the beloved patroness of Cuba, Our Lady of Charity of El Cobre.

⮜

The Mass the next day in Havana's Plaza de la Revolución was every bit as memorable. In an officially atheist land where food is doled out in small portions to the subservient, where the average monthly wage is twelve dollars, and where well-nourished toughs known as "Committees for the Defense of the Revolution" roam and control every neighborhood, more than half a million souls assembled to celebrate the Eucharist with the Bishop of Rome, while the *Comandante* and his retainers looked on.

The liturgy was magnificent. A choir of several hundred sustained by a symphonic orchestra led hymns that all seemed to know by heart, and this in a land where the Catholic faithful have been ruthlessly persecuted for almost forty years. Borrowing for the theme of his homily words of the Son of God from the Gospel of Saint Luke (4:18), the Holy Father proclaimed: "The Spirit of the Lord is upon me. He has appointed me to preach the good news to the poor, release to the captives, and liberty to the oppressed."

The crowd was electrified. We dared to hope that we were perhaps witnessing the beginning of the end of a national and spiritual tragedy.

⮜

Late in the last afternoon of our visit, I strolled the streets of Old Havana alone in a black shirt and clerical collar. Dozens stopped me to ask my blessing, and not a few knelt to receive it.

My wandering ended in the Parque Central (Central Park), a pathetic cluster of shriveled palm trees and broken stone benches. I sat on the ledge of an empty fountain basin behind a statue of José Martí, Cuba's national hero, tracing on my guidebook map the streets I had traversed.

Practice for Heaven

Looking up, I saw before me a decaying Spanish colonial edifice on which was mounted a sign that read "Hotel Inglaterra." Entering through its bronze, art-deco doors, I found inside two spacious lobbies, one of which was furnished with plastic porch chairs set around tiny tables covered with frayed, checkered tablecloths. An elderly woman played "Fascination" on a little spinet piano in the corner.

I ordered a cup of coffee from a waiter who took enormous pleasure in addressing me over and over as Padre. Leaning forward in the porch chair, I folded my hands in prayer for the "noble people" who tried to teach me their language thirty-three years earlier.

I smiled and mused to myself: the wife of the haberdasher was wrong. One of us had "made it back."

Bridgeport, May 1998

A Promise Kept

On May 5, 1791, the Polish nation issued a document entitled
A Declaration of the Assembly of Estates. It gave Poland its first
constitution and was received throughout the land with genuine
joy. In one paragraph of the declaration we read:

> So that generations yet to come might more strongly feel
> that a work so desirable [as our constitution] was, despite
> difficulties and obstacles, brought to a successful conclu-
> sion with the help of the Most High God, and so that we
> might never lose the gift of our strength and safety as a
> nation, we declare that in remembrance of this event, an
> "*ex-voto*" church [a church based on a promise or vow] is
> to be erected and consecrated to Divine Providence with
> all classes and estates participating.

Thus, a promise was made, architects were engaged, a fitting
location for the church was identified, and gifts were received
to fund the venture.

Unfortunately, however, all of this came to a halt less than
a year after the issuing of the declaration. For, in 1792, the government of Stanisław August Poniatowski, the last of the Polish
kings, and the government of Catherine the Great, the czarina
of Russia, became entangled in disputes. The result was a series

of bloody conflicts and, finally, the partition of Poland by Russia, Prussia, and Austria. Accordingly, the nation known as Poland was removed from the map of Europe from 1795 to 1918, when it gained a measure of independence for a brief period of twenty years.

⁓

On March 17, 1921, the Independent Republic of Poland renewed the nation's commitment to build a church dedicated to Divine Providence. Once again, architects were engaged, and a fitting location was identified. In 1939, Hitler's armies moved in, and when they left, Stalin's took their place. Hence, the building of the church was again deferred. Indeed, most were convinced that it was an altogether dead letter.

Józef Cardinal Glemp, the archbishop of Warsaw and the primate of Poland, was of a different mind. Accordingly, six years ago, he began the construction of the church in a neighborhood of Warsaw that the Communists had years earlier cleared with a view of creating an elegant community for their top leaders. The basement of the edifice is complete. It is massive and will serve as the foundation for the church, which is to accommodate seven thousand worshippers and be ready for services within three years.

⁓

Last year, Cardinal Glemp was in New York for a meeting with Polish-American Catholics. One afternoon he came to see me in my office on First Avenue. With undisguised delight, he informed me that the Holy Father, Pope John Paul II, wished to have me travel to Poland to inaugurate the Church of Divine Providence, inasmuch as the foundation was in place and work was soon to begin on the main body of it. On his own part, the cardinal also asked if I would be willing to address a plenary session of the Conference of Polish Catholic Bishops during my visit.

Without a moment's hesitation, I assured him that I would be more than honored to inaugurate the church and address the bishops' conference as well.

As often happens with such visits, a number of other events were added to the program. Thus, some weeks after my conversation with Cardinal Glemp, I was invited by letter to address a convocation at the University of Stefan Cardinal Wyszynski and receive an honorary Doctorate of Law. This event was set for a few hours after my priest-secretary and I arrived in Warsaw. In addition, shortly before our departure from New York, I was asked by telephone to travel to the city of Czestochowa during our visit in order to celebrate Mass at the altar of the so-called Black Madonna in the monastery of Jasna Gora. Similarly, when this became known, I was urged again by telephone to tour an exhibit concerning the history of the Jewish community in Czestochowa after the Mass in the monastery.

Amazingly, all of this, along with the inauguration of the church and the address to the conference of bishops, was somehow to be fit into three and a half days!

~

About each of these events I could write at length. The Stefan Cardinal Wyszynski University is a marvel. Six years ago, it was an academy of the Archdiocese of Warsaw for religious studies. Today, it boasts over ten thousand students and a splendid campus of impressive modern buildings.

The meeting with the conference of bishops was an eye-opener. In addition to learning of the works and initiatives of the Church in Poland, I was present to hear reports regarding their local churches by the presidents of the conferences of bishops of the nine nations that were to enter into the European Union along with Poland on the night before the inauguration of the Church of Divine Providence. What they had to say moved me deeply, especially their accounts of the trials and indignities their people had suffered under the yoke of the Soviet Union.

The Mass at the Monastery of Jasna Gora was a prayer that I shall never forget. The throng in attendance exhibited a measure of devotion unparalleled in my experience. The visit to the Jewish historical exposition was likewise an extraordinarily moving experience. An American Jew from New York, Mr. Sigmund A. Rolat, was our guide. As he pointed to the photographs of relatives of his who had lived in Czestochowa and were killed by the Nazis, one could not but profoundly feel—and share—his hurt.

It was the inauguration of the Church of Divine Providence, however, that captivated me utterly. Over what will one day be the front of the church there had been constructed a wooden wall painted blue and about three stories high. The altar for the Mass was erected under a canopy about fifty feet in front of the wall, and the wall itself was graced with a large reproduction of the Black Madonna and a ledge on which were to be placed, during the Mass, sixteen relics of traditional Polish saints and—interestingly—Saint Thérèse of Lisieux, Saint Bridget of Sweden, and Mother Teresa of Calcutta.

As we stood quietly in our places, a procession wound its way slowly through the crowd, up past the altar and toward the wall. Its participants carried with them the aforementioned relics in splendid reliquaries that vested deacons carefully set in their places on the ledge. All the while, a choir with orchestra led the thousands in the meadow surrounding the church foundation as they sang hymn after hymn.

I celebrated the Mass in Latin. The president of the Conference of Polish Catholic Bishops, Archbishop Józef Michalik, delivered the homily. The president of the Polish Republic spoke before the Mass; and at noon, also before the Mass, Pope John Paul II appeared on mammoth movie screens that could be seen by all in attendance. He was praying the Angelus with the pilgrims in the Piazza San Pietro in Rome, as he does every Sunday.

At the conclusion of the prayer he addressed the crowd assembled around the future Church of Divine Providence and ended by thanking the archbishop of New York for journeying to Poland for the celebration. As one can well imagine, I was deeply honored.

⁓

As a high school student more than fifty years ago, I had occasion to learn a few words and expressions in Polish from my classmates and friends. Whatever of this, the homily of Archbishop Michalik and the address of the Polish president were well beyond my capacity to comprehend. Thus, I had plenty of time during the inauguration ceremony to mull over what was happening and to appreciate the significance of it in the depths of my soul.

We were gathered to fulfill a commitment made 213 years earlier. I had never heard of such a thing and could not help but greatly admire my hosts. Their nation had made a vow, and they had stood by it through thick and thin.

Indeed, "thick and thin" is a monumental understatement. They had stood by it in the face of all manner of injustice, mistreatment, and oppression; and they had wavered not at all. They were grateful for the gifts the Lord had given them over the centuries, and they were expressing their gratitude on the occasion of their entering into the European Union, full of hopes for a bright, new day, economically and in every other way as well.

As I said good-bye to Cardinal Glemp at the Warsaw airport, I thanked him profusely for his hospitality and, especially, for his having given me the grace of witnessing a holy and noble promise being kept by a holy and noble people.

New York, June 2004

Missionaries

In the spring of 1982, I met several times with two Italian couples who were friends of mine in Rome in order to plan a trip to China. The travel agency offered a variety of tours, each including eight or nine stops. One of our number was particularly interested in visiting the petrified forest outside of Kunming in the Southwest of China. He had read a book about it and was struck by the fact that few from the West had made the effort to see it.

The argument against our going to the petrified forest was the need to stop on the way in a city by the name of Nanning, which most guidebooks declared to be of little interest. Nonetheless, ceding to the desire of our companion, we agreed to include Kunming, the petrified forest, and the unavoidable Nanning in our itinerary.

We arrived in Nanning on August 9 and were lodged in a hotel that was at one time the residence of the French consul general. It faced a park and was graced by an imposing porch that stretched across the entire length of its façade.

The first evening, the five of us stood on the porch of our hotel after supper, admiring the park and chatting. The conversation was soon interrupted by the arrival of five young Chinese men, whom I gauged to be in their late twenties. Each had with him an ungainly, black bicycle such as one sees throughout China.

The leader of the group, a bright-eyed fellow with prominent teeth and ill-fitting glasses, asked if we spoke English. I replied that I did and that my friends understood it quite well.

"Excellent," he cried. "May I invite you to the home of the wealthiest woman in Nanning for tea and talk?"

My friends and I discussed the invitation among ourselves and finally decided, with some apprehension, to accept it. Thus, we followed the young men as they walked their bicycles around the edge of the park to a house whose architecture was strangely similar to that of our hotel. It had a porch across the front, and from the street one could look inside through a large double door to see a lady of advanced years sitting in front of a foot-pedal sewing machine. She was identified for us as "the wealthiest woman in Nanning."

We entered the house and were seated on narrow wooden chairs. Looking around the room, we spied four young ladies crouched near the rear wall and a fifth sitting on a steel bench before a second foot-pedal sewing machine. The five ladies were evidently friends of the five Chinese men, the leader of whom gestured to the two sewing machines with courtly respect. He hoped we were aware that we were the guests of a manifestly well-to-do personage.

All five of the young men spoke English reasonably well. They had learned it, they explained, "from BBC discs" and "at our academy." None knew Italian. Hence, I served as a translator for my group, and the five young men took turns translating for the Chinese ladies.

Shortly after tea had been served in the familiar covered cups, the conversation turned to politics. With much laughing and searching for synonyms, we explained how people in the West rule themselves, using the Italian Republic as our exemplar. We told about the president of the republic who had replaced the king as the head of state. We went into detail about the Senate and the Chamber of Deputies, the lower house of Parliament in Italy. And we made much of the prime minister and the manner in which he and the president of the republic are elected.

In fact, as the evening wore on, we conducted a mock election in which I was chosen president of the republic and the leader of the Chinese men became prime minister. Over and again, he reminded us that, by my own admission, the president of the republic had little to do, while the prime minister made all-important decisions for the nation. With each repetition of this insight into Italian civics, the room rocked with laughter.

Late that night, we returned to our hotel. We had had an unexpectedly delightful adventure about which we could not stop talking.

~

The next evening my travel companions and I again went out on the hotel porch for air after supper. There waiting for us were the five young Chinese men. The wealthiest woman in Nanning would be pleased to have us to her home again, we were told; and tonight she would be serving "not only tea but also biscuits." We accepted the invitation without a moment's hesitation.

As soon as the tea and biscuits had been passed around, the man with the prominent teeth and ill-fitting glasses initiated the conversation with a subject that had evidently been agreed upon by his colleagues and their lady friends beforehand. When he and I were elected prime minister and president of the republic respectively, he noted, we had "sworn an oath to God."

"Tell us about God," he said.

The Italian couples and I took counsel about how best to answer. We settled on an approach. I would do most of the talking because of my knowledge of English, and they, by asking questions, would make sure that I was being understood.

According to the plan, I started with the creation of man and woman, moved on to their sin, and at length came to Jesus Christ, His birth, His miracles, His death on the Cross, His Resurrection, His command that we love God with all our hearts and our neighbor as ourselves, and His founding of the Church to continue His work on earth.

At the time, I had been a priest for twenty-four years and had preached many a sermon, but never had I experienced such undivided attention. The first night, the wealthiest woman in Nanning had sat more or less impassive at her sewing machine. Tonight, she was clearly enthralled. Often she surveyed the room to be sure that the young Chinese, especially the young ladies, were not missing a word.

"Was Jesus Christ truly the Son of God?" we were asked. "Why did His Father in Heaven not wait until Jesus Christ was an old man before He had to die on the Cross?" "Did someone take care of His mother after Jesus Christ went to Heaven?" "Do all except Chinese people know about Jesus Christ?" "Why is there no mention of Jesus Christ on BBC discs?" "Do all followers of Jesus Christ love God with all their hearts and their neighbor as themselves?" "Will someone be coming sometime to Nanning to tell us about Jesus Christ?"

⁀

Back at the hotel, my friends and I stood on the porch, so moved by the events of the evening that, unlike the night before, we did not know what to say to one another. There seemed to be nothing to do but pray.

Accordingly, in the manner of Offertory petitions at Mass, I began: "That we Catholics may never forget that we are a missionary people, bound to tell the world of our Lord and Savior, Jesus Christ; let us pray to the Lord." All responded: "Lord, hear our prayer."

And I went on: "That dedicated missionaries in great numbers come forward to preach the Gospel to every nation; let us pray to the Lord." Again, all responded: "Lord, hear our prayer."

I was about to formulate a third petition when one of the Italian men interrupted me. "That all missionaries," he whispered, "in their missionary labors know the kind of deep, spiritual fulfillment I have experienced this evening, let us pray to the Lord."

In the heavy, nighttime air of a summer in southwest China, five voices were once more carried into the heavens.

"Lord, hear our prayer," they begged.

Bridgeport, October 1990

Dublin's Fair and Holy City

Each week I join Mr. Rob Astorino for a one-hour program on *The Catholic Channel* on Sirius/XM Satellite Radio. Rob is the channel's program director and acts as my interlocutor for the show. The format of what we have come to call "A Conversation with the Cardinal" is a discussion between Mr. Astorino and me on questions of Scripture, Tradition, theology, and events in the Archdiocese of New York and in the Church across the world. It also includes responses to questions sent us by mail, over the telephone, by fax, and by e-mail.[6]

Some weeks ago, I reported that I had been in Rome for meetings at the Vatican and later in Dublin for my annual retreat. Shortly thereafter, I received a letter from a man living in one of the "Upper Counties" of the archdiocese with a very courteously lodged complaint. He reminded me that when I leave New York for whatever reason, I usually, upon return, describe on *The Catholic Channel* what I had seen and done.

"You were in Rome and you told of your visit to the church where Saint Paul had been a prisoner, and you told it both on Sirius Satellite Radio and in an article in *Catholic New York*," he

---

[6] Cardinal Egan founded *The Catholic Channel* in 2006. Rob Astorino was program director from 2006 to 2009.

wrote. "But not a word about your retreat in Dublin. How about a report about 'Dublin's Fair City'? With a name like Egan, you have to have at least a wee bit of Irish blood running through your veins."

I examined my conscience and decided that my correspondent was right. What follows is an effort to make amends.

⌒

The doctor who replaced my left knee years ago told me that I should try to take a daily walk so as to keep the knee in operation. For me, this is no easy task because of an always overcrowded calendar. In Dublin, however, I followed my doctor's orders, made my way each day on foot to visit a church or shrine, and came away both informed and inspired.

One Sunday, having celebrated Mass very early in the morning, I walked over to Saint Mary's Pro-Cathedral for Mass there at ten o'clock. The two ancient and storied Catholic cathedrals of Dublin — Saint Patrick's and Christ Church — were, of course, taken over by the Church of England in the 1500s, and it was not until the early 1800s that Catholics were even permitted to build themselves a new cathedral. It was to be on O'Connell Street, one of the principal thoroughfares of the city. This, however, was disallowed by the Protestant establishment. Thus, Saint Mary's Pro-Cathedral is located on Marlborough Street in a less elegant area known as Monto.

As the Mass was about to conclude, a priest entered the pulpit to announce that the pro-cathedral's celebrated Palestrina Chorus, which once included in its ranks the great Irish tenor John McCormack, was on vacation. Its place for the noonday Mass this one Sunday would be taken, he said, by the Chorus of the City of Dublin. I decided to stay for yet another liturgy.

The pews of the pro-cathedral were two-thirds full for the nine o'clock Mass and packed for the Mass at noon. I was deeply taken by every element of the celebration. The ceremonies were dignified, the homily was insightful, and the choir was a delight. Indeed, the music was so outstanding that, at the conclusion of the final chorus, the congregation broke into applause.

What impressed me most, however, was the age of the congregation. I had been led to expect only the elderly. But such was not the case. Men and women in their twenties, thirties, and forties were in the majority, many with children in tow.

When I returned to the religious house where I was staying, the morning newspaper was under my door. Its front page featured the priestly ordination of three young men in the pro-cathedral the day before. There could not have been a more encouraging climax to my visit to Saint Mary's.

The Carmelite Church known as Whitefriars was another delightful destination for my daily walks. It is immense and most deserving of a visit from anyone coming to Dublin. In the sixteenth century, it was seized by King Henry VIII and closed until 1827, when the Carmelite Fathers, the Whitefriars, reopened and restored it.

On a weekday, I attended a noon Mass there. Well over two hundred men and women were at prayer in a moving liturgy enhanced by a fascinating homily that focused on the life and work of Saint Benedict of Nursia, the founder of Western monasticism and the saint of the day.

On the right as I entered I discovered an extraordinarily large shrine, whose centerpiece was a tall, carved-oak statue of the Madonna that is alleged to be the only such image to have escaped the fury of the Tudors. As I was about to move into a nearby pew, my attention was caught by another shrine on the opposite wall, whose centerpiece was a wooden pillar into which a relic of Saint Valentine had been inserted. (The relic was, I learned, given to the church in 1837 by Pope Gregory XVI.)

Next to the pillar stood a rather ungainly wooden table. On it lay a huge open book bound in leather and accompanied by a sign inviting the faithful to write a prayer to Saint Valentine in its pages. There were several such prayers written on the two pages open before me.

Another, though, was written on a half sheet of note paper and lodged in the book's binding. It read: "Holy Saint Valentine, help me to thank the Lord for my wonderful wife."

When the Mass was over, I passed a long line of men and women waiting to go to Confession and finally moved out onto the street. The sun was shining splendidly after a "soft" rain, and all seemed right with the world.

Returning to New York, I had to give a talk the following week to a group of young couples in one of our archdiocesan marriage-preparation programs. I opened by telling of the prayer I had discovered in Dublin's Whitefriars Church. Once I had recited it, the talk took off on its own.

~

Trinity College is neither a church nor a shrine. It is, though, built on land once owned by Augustinian monks, from whom it was confiscated in 1592, on orders from Queen Elizabeth I.

What no Catholic visitor to this institution will want to miss is to be found in a building on the campus known as the Old Library. It is the *Book of Kells*, one of the most treasured books in the world, dated around A.D. 800 and containing the four

Gospels, several Prefaces for Mass, and other assorted prayers, all in Latin and all embellished with some of the most intricate designs the human mind has ever devised. I went to see it first and foremost for reasons spiritual, since one cannot inspect its pages without sensing that it is a prayer in art and a testament to a deep and abiding love for the Word of God.

The volume is made up of 680 pages and was produced in the monastery of Saint Columcille of the island of Iona. Early in the 800s, it was taken to County Meath, where it was famously stolen in 1007. Found buried three months later, it was restored and finally brought to Trinity College in 1654.

Two pages were open for me to inspect. The most elaborately decorated was the title page of the Gospel according to Saint Matthew colored in bright red, yellow, and orange, and so filled with flourishes of all kinds that the eye does not know where to settle. Adorned throughout with countless images of angels, animals, and flowers, the book expresses an incredible reverence for the Word of God and the prayers of His Church. It is a masterwork of both art and holiness.

Shortly before I left Dublin, a young priest friend told me that I absolutely had to "check out" the Kilmainham Gaol (Jail), the infamous institution in which so many Irish men and women were held and killed because of love of and loyalty to their land and faith.

"Take the tour," he insisted, "and at the first stop you will see why this place is a must for a Catholic, and especially a Catholic priest."

He was right beyond all doubt. The first room to which our group was taken by our very articulate and very Catholic guide was a windowless chapel whose altar and other liturgical appurtenances had been fashioned out of wood by prisoners who were being horrendously mistreated and, in not a few instances, slowly starved to death.

When the guide finished her description of the place, two young men from the United States in jackets announcing the university they were attending or had attended went down on their knees, made the Sign of the Cross, and remained kneeling, heads bowed. Several others followed suit, as did I.

In all frankness, I must confess that I listened to the rest of the tour guide's presentation with a certain indifference, for I did not want to lose the deep-down holiness that had taken hold of me in the chapel.

Thankfully, it remained until we completed the last stop of our tour, an exercise yard where, after the Easter Rising of 1916, a host of Ireland's most revered heroes were executed. There was nothing in the yard apart from two black crosses, the first of them marking where twelve rebel commanders were killed after being pushed up against a pile of burlap bags; and the second marking where the renowned Irish patriot James Connolly, sick unto death, was killed while strapped to a chair. The crosses spoke volumes about so much pain borne by so many for so long.

⁓

I left the jail in haste so as to make a stop at one of the two formerly Catholic cathedrals of Dublin, Christ Church. The reason was my desire to say a prayer near the reliquary that is said to contain the heart of Saint Lawrence O'Toole, who became the first archbishop of Dublin in 1162, participated in the Third Lateran Ecumenical Council in Rome, and gallantly defended the rights of the Church against the assaults of the ruthless King Henry II.

As I waited to pay for a book about the saint that I was purchasing for the pastor of the parish of Saint Lawrence O'Toole in

Brewster, New York, I noted that an entire wall of the vestibule of the cathedral was devoted to the sale of religious articles. Hanging on it were dozens upon dozens of rosaries of all sizes and colors.

I could not help but suspect that, from his place in Heaven, Saint Lawrence is often amused and perhaps even heartened by this feature in the Protestant house of worship where he is remembered and venerated. Certainly, I was from my place in Dublin's Fair — and Holy — City.

New York, August 2008

Four Languages in June

It was June of 1976. With a group of Italian friends, I was on a tour of the Czech Socialist Republic. There were fourteen in our party, and for most of us, this was a second journey together behind the Iron Curtain.

In Prague, our guide was a tall, rather stately lady. She dutifully led us from museum to museum, from palace to palace, from church to church, repeating in fluent but heavily accented Italian the standard line prepared for all official guides by the government tourist office.

In churches in Communist countries of the time, a stop before a shrine dedicated to Mary was commonly accompanied by a commentary of this kind for the tourist: "This structure has to do with the so-called Virgin Mary, whom Catholics adore as though she were a god or goddess. It was designed by So-and-so and was for hundreds of years before the revolution a center of Catholic superstition."

The guide who was assigned to us appeared to be extremely tired and burdened. Hence, our group soon got into the habit of respectfully hearing her official remarks and then listening attentively to a jeweler from Milan, who was a member of the group, as he read what his Italian guidebook had to say about what we were seeing.

The jeweler frequently kidded me, the *Monsignore*, about matters religious, clearly seeking to communicate that he did not take his Catholic Faith overly much to heart. Thus, none of us suspected that he was making up what he seemed to be reading from his guidebook about a shrine dedicated to Mary in the Cathedral of Saint Vitus in Prague, after our guide had finished some particularly ugly, government-authorized comments.

"This altar," he announced, "was built as a testimony of the Catholic faithful to their belief in the divinity of Jesus Christ and the holiness of His Mother, the Virgin Mary. It is meant to remind us that God is holy and expects us to be holy, too."

"Here, *Monsignore*," the jeweler continued, "read it for us in English." He handed me the guidebook and pointed to a place on the page. Nothing of what he had allegedly read was there to be found.

Still, realizing what the jeweler was up to, I took the guidebook and "read" in English: "This altar was built as a testimony of the Catholic faithful to their belief in the divinity of Jesus Christ and the holiness of His Mother, the Virgin Mary. It is meant to remind us that God is holy and expects us to be holy, too."

In our party was an Italian professor of French from the University of Perugia, a lady of about sixty years of age. She too often made it clear to all in a rather elegant and playful manner that she was not "fanatically" Catholic.

All the same, she intuited what was happening, seized the guidebook from my hand, and finding the imaginary place on the page, recited the supposed passage in a classic French that would have made even Flaubert jealous.

"This altar was built as a testimony of the Catholic faithful to their belief in the divinity of Jesus Christ and the holiness of His

Mother, the Virgin Mary," she declaimed. "It is meant to remind us that God is holy and expects us to be holy, too."

We were all so thoroughly enjoying our little game of reciting with impunity Catholic doctrine about the Lord and His Mother in the capital of the most bitterly anti-Catholic regime of the Communist empire that we had not noticed that our guide was slumped in a narrow wooden pew some few yards away, quietly sobbing.

"*Signore*," she called through her tears to the Italian jeweler, "could you kindly repeat that section from your guidebook. I was not able to catch it all."

The French professor handed the guidebook back to the Italian jeweler. By now he, too, was crying. In fact, we all were.

"This altar was built as a testimony of the Catholic faithful to their belief in the divinity of Jesus Christ and the holiness of His Mother, the Virgin Mary," he whispered. But he could not go on. Emotion had overtaken him. He just stared at the grimy marble floor and wept.

The guide continued for him: "It is meant to remind us that God is holy and expects us to be holy, too."

The group walked silently out of the cathedral, not daring to look at one another. The tour was over. We invited the guide to our hotel for coffee. She could not come. She had to go home to her husband, who was not well.

⁓

We returned to the hotel, ordered coffee, and sat down in the drab lobby. The Italian jeweler looked at me with the air of someone who had just been vanquished in a game of cards.

"Well, *Monsignore*," said he, "you must have enjoyed all of that catechism talk about the Madonna repeated in three languages in the cathedral of Prague."

Practice for Heaven

The French professor did not allow me to reply.

"Four languages, Monsieur," she interjected, "Italian, English, French, and ... tears." With that she rose, assumed a tone of declamation, and recited the words of the Mother of God in her Magnificat:

> *My soul magnifies the Lord, and my spirit rejoices*
> > *in God my Savior,*
> *for He has regarded the low estate of His handmaiden.*
> *Behold, henceforth, all generations will call me blessed.*
> > (Luke 1:46–48)

Then, averting her eyes so that no one might detect what she was feeling, she hurriedly left the lobby.

❧

I do not know how many of us cried again once we were safely in our respective hotel rooms. At least one did, and this was not the last time that tears came to my eyes when recalling four languages in honor of Mary in the cathedral of Prague one day in June.

Bridgeport, June 1990

Another Star

Twenty years ago, for the first time, I visited Prague, the capital of what was then called the People's Republic of Czechoslovakia. The Soviet army occupied the land, and the Soviet government was siphoning off whatever resources it could in order to sustain its tottering empire. Nonetheless, Prague retained much of its traditional charm. With a modicum of effort one could look past the general disrepair of things and imagine quite well what this celebrated capital of Bohemia had once been and what it might one day be.

This past summer I returned to Prague, now the capital of what is known as the Czech Republic. With lay friends I once again explored the ancient Cathedral of Saint Vitus, the massive Hradčany Castle, and the splendid Stahov Abbey. We ate Bohemian strudel in the Town Hall Square. We even heard an opera by Mozart in a surprisingly small theater where the composer had first conducted it.

For me, however, the high point of the visit was a brief encounter on the Charles Bridge, which spans the Vltava or Moldau River, dividing the city in two.

❦

The Charles Bridge was constructed in the second half of the 1300s by Charles IV, the king of Bohemia and later the Holy

Roman Emperor. It is 570 yards long and 33 feet wide, closed to vehicular traffic, and adorned with thirty huge statues of saints, fifteen on either side. In front of each of the statues artists have set up stands at which they hawk paintings, etchings, and engravings of Prague and especially of the Charles Bridge. On a cool, cloudless day, I stood before the statue of Saint John Nepomucene while bargaining in my faltering German over a small engraving of the Cathedral of Saint Vitus.

An American man of perhaps forty years of age tugged at my sleeve. "When you're finished," he said, "would you mind asking the lady how much she wants for this engraving?"

I did as he requested. She responded 170 korunas (about $6.50), the same price she was asking of me. I suggested she make it 150 korunas if we each bought one. With some hesitation, she agreed.

As our purchases were being wrapped, first in cellophane and then in heavy blue paper, the man shouted to his son on the other side of the bridge not to stray too far. He was a boy of nine or ten in baggy pants, running shoes, and a baseball cap with its peak turned toward the back.

"I wonder who that is," the man said to me, pointing toward the statue in front of us.

"Saint John Nepomucene," I replied, "the patron saint of confessors; that is, of priests who hear the confessions of the faithful."

"I bet you're a Catholic priest," he observed with a knowing smile.

"Yes," I responded. "And you, are you a Catholic?" I asked.

"Well, sort of," he answered, "but I've not been much into confession of late."

"You ought to buy an engraving of the saint and take it home with you," I suggested. "Saint John Nepomucene will help you back into the confession habit."

The man was clearly uncomfortable with this last remark. He turned toward the lady who was laboriously wrapping the engravings, urged her on with a gesture of his hand, and turned back to me.

"Why is the saint carrying a palm branch?" he asked in an evident effort to change the direction of the conversation.

"Because the palm branch is a symbol of martyrdom, and Saint John Nepomucene was martyred, thrown into the river from this very bridge by the son of Emperor Charles IV when he refused to reveal what was told to him by a penitent in confession," I explained. "He wasn't officially enrolled among the saints until the end of the 1700s, after four extraordinary miracles were attributed to him. They are symbolized by the four large stars attached to his halo."

"Really?" the man exclaimed, looking again impatiently in the direction of the lady still engaged in wrapping our engravings. "And why the oversized crucifix in his arms?"

"Because," I replied, "the artist is eager to make it clear that the priest in confession does not act on his own. Far from it! The forgiveness comes from the Lord, Who simply uses the priest as an instrument of His grace. It is the crucified Savior Who in the final analysis does the forgiving."

"Yes, of course," the man remarked, "but it's hard for most ordinary folks to see it that way."

"Well," I insisted, "buy an engraving of the saint, bring it back to the States, and let Father John Nepomucene help make everything crystal clear."

The man laughed nervously. "That would take another miracle, I'm afraid, and a big one at that," he said. "I better not get the saint involved and then disappoint him."

The lady finished her work. The man shook my hand and, in a flash, headed across the bridge toward his son, the elegantly wrapped engraving protruding from a side pocket of his windbreaker.

⌒

I continued my stroll along the Charles Bridge, stopping for a prayer before each of the remaining statues and casually inspecting the wares of the artists at their stands. As I was about to leave the bridge for the Old Town Tower, where I agreed to join my friends at noon, a boy of nine or ten in baggy pants, running shoes, and a baseball cap with its peak turned toward the back ran up to me.

"This is from my dad," he announced, panting. "He told me to tell you that he had bought one just like it for himself."

Before I was able to say "thank you," the boy scooted off toward the center of the bridge. I could see my friends outside the Old Town Tower waving anxiously in my direction. Nevertheless, I carefully undid the cellophane and blue paper wrappings from the object in my hands. As I had hoped, it was an engraving of the statue of Saint John Nepomucene.

My friends were now shouting to gain my attention. Hence, I could not return to the statue on the bridge. All the same, I was quite sure that if I had, I would have found another large star attached to its halo.

Bridgeport, October 1996

"Fiat"

Husband and wife, they were the proprietors of a little shop in Rome that sold postcards, guidebooks, and lithographs of churches and monuments. I first met them in 1973 and occasionally joined them in their apartment for dinners and family celebrations.

In 1976, the couple made a pilgrimage to Lourdes, a town in southwestern France where the Virgin Mary was reported to have appeared in 1858 to Bernadette Soubirous, a girl of fourteen years of age who later became a religious Sister and, still later, a canonized saint. Shortly after their return to Rome, I was invited to their home. The husband suffered from chronic back pain, and the wife from occasional attacks of asthma. Both indicated that they were feeling better after their pilgrimage, and with much warmth and kindness presented me with a rosary they had purchased there.

It was a rather unusual rosary. In place of the medal that ordinarily joins the five sets of beads to the four beads that lead to the crucifix, this rosary was fitted with a metal and plastic bubble containing a drop of water.

"It's water from the grotto where Bernadette saw the Virgin," I was told, and I thanked the couple profusely.

Practice for Heaven

Later that same year, a priest friend of mine from the Diocese of Sioux Falls and I arranged to join a group of Italians for a week-long tour of Hungary. Because of the religious persecution in that Communist-controlled nation, we obtained new passports that identified us as "professors" and included photographs of us in open-collar shirts. Keenly aware of the political situation, we repeatedly reminded each other never to say anything negative about the Communist regime during the tour and not to bring with us anything of a religious nature.

One afternoon, in the course of our exploring Budapest, we passed by the American embassy in which József Cardinal Mind-szenty, the primate of Poland, had taken refuge in 1956 after a popular uprising against the Communist government was violently beaten down. We stayed on the opposite side of the street, taking in the passing scene with as casual an air as we could manage. On the street, two sullen soldiers paced back and forth with rifles in their hands. Across the street, the sidewalk was strewn with cut flowers that courageous Hungarians continued to leave under the apartment in which the cardinal had resided until 1971.

Without thinking, I put my hand into my pocket to take out the rosary that I was accustomed to carry there. It was the one that contained the water from Lourdes. Suddenly, I realized that I had unwittingly brought with me a very religious article that I should have left in Rome.

As we walked away from the embassy, I again put my hand into my pocket and nervously began to recite my Rosary in silence. Curiously, I could not decide on the object of my prayer. It was widely assumed that Hungary would never be free as long as the Soviet Union had the "bomb."

Likewise, it was widely conceded that Cardinal Mindszenty's reputation, which the Communists had been doing all they could to besmirch, would never be restored. Indeed, a rather broad spectrum of the press in Europe had been for some time waging a campaign to soil it by suggesting that at some point in his life he may have had Fascist leanings.

Accordingly, he, too, seemed to be beyond the reach of my conversation with the Lord. Thus, as we made our way through the streets of Budapest, my only prayer was that of Mary when she was asked by her heavenly Father to be the Mother of His Son according to the flesh. With the utmost of humility and courage, she simply acceded to His holy will, not asking what that might entail and not even considering the cost.

"*Fiat*," she said. "Let it be done."

As I was completing the final decade of my troublesome Rosary, an old gray-stone church came into view, a side door of which stood partly open. My priest friend and I went in and looked around, as though we were simply uninterested tourists. In a dark corner of the building, I took my rosary out of my pocket and allowed it to slip into one of the dusty pews.

Once outside, my priest friend looked at me with suspicion and inquired if something was amiss.

"Not now," I replied with no small measure of relief. "Not now."

⁓

During the first week of May in 1991, I had the honor of serving as chaplain for 162 pilgrims to Lourdes from Connecticut, New York, and New Jersey. Throughout our stay, the weather was cold and rainy. Thus, one afternoon, as I returned to my hotel from the Grotto of the Virgin, I stopped in a tiny café for a hot cup of "coffee with milk."

Before entering I had bought a French newspaper that I used to read in the early 1960s, when I was teaching in a seminary in Rome. It was always well written, but also quite radical in its politics and unashamedly anti-Catholic as well.

On the front page, "above the fold," as they say, I spied an article that announced that the mortal remains of Cardinal Mindszenty, who died in 1975, had been transferred to Hungary from Austria, where he had lived in exile since 1971, when he was spirited out to the American embassy in Budapest.

"Now that atheistic Communism has lost its stranglehold on Hungary," the article stated, "the body of the martyred Cardinal can be properly buried with all the honors that are his due." And this event, the article continued, "signals the return of the Hungarian nation to Europe, to freedom, and to democracy."

Curiously, the article went even so far as to recall that, shortly after his consecration as a bishop, the cardinal had been imprisoned "by Fascists," a fact that most reporters and editorial-page writers had been careful not to share with their readers throughout the 1960s and 1970s.

⁓

I set the newspaper aside and sipped my coffee slowly. Fifteen years earlier, I had had little hope for the liberation of the Hungarian people and the recognition of their cardinal primate for the heroic shepherd of souls and noble son of Hungary that he was.

Thus, as I spoke with my Lord while walking through the streets of Budapest, my only prayer was that of Mary in her marvelously uncomplicated response to the Angel Gabriel when he announced the will of God in her regard: "Fiat," which is to say, "Let it be done."

Sitting in the French café over a cup of coffee, I suddenly came to realize with a clarity never before attained that Mary's simple, direct, and humble prayer when she was asked to be the Mother of God is to be my prayer in all circumstances of life, favorable as well as unfavorable. It is not to be prayed only when tragedies take hold and hopes are dashed. It is, rather, meant to be called upon in any and every significant situation in which we find ourselves.

In all settings and at all times, our intention, our desire, and our focus is, in the plainest of terms, to do the will of our Creator and Lord. Nothing is more basic. Nothing is more certain. Our lives, from birth to death, are to be an unbroken series, a concatenation, if you will, of fiats, courageous, loving fiats.

I paid the waiter for my coffee, walked out into the rain, crossed a slippery, stone-paved street, and entered one of Lourdes' many religious-goods stores.

"I am looking for a rosary that contains water from the Grotto of the Virgin," I told an elderly clerk behind a well-worn counter. She beckoned me into a storeroom and drew from a glass-covered case a rosary very much like the one I had abandoned in the church in Budapest.

"It's a gift that can inspire the most fervent of prayers and the most thoughtful of meditations," she declared with a flair I had not expected. "About this, Reverend Father, I am altogether sure," she added with a knowing smile.

"And so am I," I responded with a smile no less knowing.

Bridgeport, June 1991

Enlightenment

"I'm a Catholic," he whispered, looking down at his shoes, "but I don't know anything about my faith. I went to public schools and just a few catechism classes before First Holy Communion and . . ." His voice trailed off. "And I don't have a clue about the Church I think I love," he added mournfully.

Well and Always

The cardinal archbishop of Chicago came lumbering down the stairs with an uncharacteristic smile on his face. "Good morning, Father, and Happy Thanksgiving," he said. "I have a little something for you."

With that he handed me two small, cloth-bound books, each about seven by five inches, and both written by Reverend Raoul Plus, S.J. One was entitled *How to Pray Well* and the other, *How to Pray Always.*

"You will enjoy these wonderful little volumes," he announced. "They are filled with spiritual wisdom."

I thanked him, helped him with his overcoat, and followed him out to a waiting car. We were on our way to Holy Name Cathedral for Thanksgiving Mass at 9:00 a.m.

～

Ordinarily, the cardinal, whose secretary I was, preferred to ride in silence. I had learned early in our relationship not to initiate conversations.

This day, however, he was all talk. He would be going to the home of relatives for Thanksgiving dinner, he reported. This cousin would be there. This other would not. His priest nephew would arrive late. His youngest niece would sing for the family.

And on and on. I could scarcely recognize the ordinarily somber archbishop of Chicago.

When the Mass was finished, I wished His Eminence a pleasant day, left the cathedral by a side door, and hurried toward the subway. It was to take me to an elevated train which, in turn, would bring me home to Thanksgiving dinner with my family in a western suburb of the Windy City. At my side I had a small suitcase into which I had packed the cassock and surplice I had worn for Mass, my Breviary, the two books the cardinal had given me, and a rather elaborately wrapped box of chocolates for my mother.

In the last car of the elevated train there were only two other passengers. They were women who appeared to be in their late sixties. They sat together across the aisle and two rows behind me, chatting and clearly enjoying the bumpy journey.

I opened my suitcase, extracted my Breviary, and set myself to reading the Office of the day. After a few minutes, the women stopped their chatting. One cleared her throat and addressed me.

"My sister and I," she said, "have been wondering, Reverend, what it is that you are reading."

"Is it the Bible?" the other inquired.

"Not exactly," I answered. "It's a Breviary, which is full of passages from the Bible, but contains also readings from Fathers of the Church and brief biographies of saints as well."

I rose from my seat and handed the Breviary to the first sister.

"It's one of four volumes," I explained. "Each day of the year has its own arrangement of Bible passages, readings, and prayers, and what is established for each day is read by all priests and many monks and nuns across the world. We call it the Divine Office, which is to say a kind of holy obligation or duty."

The first sister handed the Breviary to the other, paused, and asked why everyone is required to read the same thing.

"It all started very early in the history of the Church," I replied. "Already in the 400s monks were living together and praying together several times a day. When in later centuries more and more were leaving their monasteries at least for a time to preach the Gospel in distant lands, it was agreed that they would recite while they were away the same prayers that their confrères were reciting back home. In this way, a missionary in Germany who had left his monastery in Italy, for example, would sense himself spiritually united to his brother monks, and supported and strengthened by them too.

"Before long," I went on, "Church authorities directed priests and nuns to follow the lead of the monks. The same Divine Office was to be recited by all who had given their lives completely to the service of the Lord, no matter where in the world. And we are doing precisely this even today."

The second sister closed my Breviary and handed it back to me. "How lovely!" she exclaimed. "I think praying that way is just beautiful. But, Reverend, I must confess that I am not at all good at praying." She hesitated a moment and then went on. "And neither is my sister. I think it's like playing the piano or violin. You have to start early in life and stick at it. Otherwise . . ."

"Otherwise," the first sister interrupted in a tone of self-depreciation, "you end up semi-pagans like us."

I opened my suitcase, placed the Breviary inside, and took out the two books by Father Plus. In the process the box of chocolates fell to the floor and bounced under the seat behind me. Having recovered it and hurriedly pushed it into my suitcase, I gave *How to Pray Well* to one sister and *How to Pray Always* to the other.

"Just this morning," I announced, "I was presented with these books by the cardinal. I have not read them myself. Yet, judging from their titles and what the cardinal told me about them, I suspect you might find them interesting. You would make my Thanksgiving if you would do me the honor of accepting them. I can easily obtain a new set."

The sisters demurred at first but finally acquiesced to my offer after I had written my name and address on a card that one of them had in her purse. As they hurried off the train at their station, each with a book in hand, I felt like one of those resourceful missionary monks of ages past. My holiday was off to a splendid start.

On the Friday after Thanksgiving, I went at lunchtime to a Catholic bookstore in the center of town and purchased a new set of Father Plus's books. It would not be well if the cardinal were to learn that I had given away his gift so shortly after receiving it.

The following Tuesday, however, His Eminence stopped me on the way to breakfast to hand me a box of chocolates with *How to Pray Well* and *How to Pray Always* fastened to it with a festive bow.

"Two ladies left this with Sister last night," he declared with a quizzical look in his eye. "They gave her this card as well," he added. "I trust that all of this makes sense to you."

I opened the card. It read as follows: "After Thanksgiving dinner, we read both of your books cover to cover. We then prayed together for the first time in a long time. We told the Lord we hoped you would always enjoy reading your holy book along with all the priests, monks, and nuns in the world, and we even prayed that your mother's chocolates weren't crushed when she opened the box."

The card was signed: "Two semi-pagans who need to pray well and always."

Bridgeport, December 1993

Succession

The letter was a delight. My correspondent was leaving Connecticut to take up residence in South America. He wrote to thank me for having confirmed two of his children and to tell me of "the countless kindnesses" he and his family had received from the priests of their parish.

A postscript was added. The night before he penned his letter, my correspondent had heard a Catholic radio program on the subject of Apostolic succession. He wanted to know if I had ever treated "this intriguing doctrine" in my sermons, noting that it was a subject of particular interest to him because he was "a convert from a Christian denomination in which Apostolic succession is totally unknown."

⌒

To prepare a fitting reply, I took from my bookshelf a textbook entitled *De Ecclesia* (Concerning the Church) written in Latin by a Spanish professor who had taught my class the course on the Church during our first year as seminarians in Rome.

The professor's name was Reverend Timotheus Zapelena, S.J., and the explanation of Apostolic succession that he provided in the second volume of his treatise on the Church was crystal clear. Saint Peter and the other Apostles were "mere mortals," he observed. Hence, once the Lord had determined the basic structure of His Church with "Peter and the eleven" as her official and essential teachers, sanctifiers, and shepherds, it was obvious that He intended that there be others who, over centuries, would take their place, which is to say, "succeed them."

These, of course, are the bishops of the one, holy, catholic, and apostolic Church, Father Zapelena announced with customary aplomb.

To demonstrate, however, that the People of God had always understood this and had, moreover, always recognized the bishops of the Church as those whom the Lord intended to succeed the Apostles, the immensely learned Jesuit professor marshaled an impressive array of statements by the Fathers of the early Church.

Well do I recall his reciting many of them in class by heart and with evident pleasure. Among them were Saint Clement of Rome, Saint Ignatius of Antioch, Saint Irenaeus, Saint Augustine, Saint Gregory the Great, and a host of others.

With a certain measure of nostalgia, I again studied what Father Zapelena wrote about Apostolic succession in his book, including a kind of sidebar (volume 2, page 11) that brought back vivid memories of his teaching style. It concerned a Christian sect that came into existence in Scotland in the mid-1800s, under the inspiration of a deposed Presbyterian minister by the name of Edward Irving.

Irving, who counted among his friends such literary lights as Thomas Carlyle, Charles Lamb, and Samuel Taylor Coleridge, was convinced that nonhierarchical denominations with no connection to the Apostles needed to be "re-constituted" according to what he called "the mind of God," and by this he meant that they needed to be endowed with some form of Apostolic succession.

To achieve this, Irving declared that he was going to choose twelve new "apostles," one of them being himself. Curiously, however, like many of the more radical Evangelicals of his era, he was somehow convinced that the world was going to come to an end in 1900. Accordingly, he proclaimed that his "apostles" should not have, and would not even need, successors.

~

In class, Father Zapelena had great fun recounting the story of Irving to the hundreds of seminarians who sat before him in Rome's Gregorian University. "These British," he intoned, "are hard to fathom. They wanted Apostolic succession but no Apostolic successors. How silly is that?"

The seminarians joined in the merriment, eagerly urging their elderly professor on as he warmed to his theme.

"Now, don't you Germans laugh," he playfully chided the German sector of the gigantic lecture hall in which we were gathered. "And don't you Americans either. In both of your nations the Irvingites still have churches and congregations, and they call themselves — I tell you no lie — the Catholic Apostolic Church."

His eyes darted around the hall.

"You doubt me?" he asked. "Well, when you Germans and you Americans return to your native lands, look into it. Two sets of apostles, the one chosen by Jesus Christ and the other chosen by Edward Irving; and according to Irving, two sets of nonsuccessors, though succession was, again according to Irving, obviously not needed. Now, where does that leave us?" He leaned into his microphone and answered his own query. "Nowhere, absolutely nowhere, except to two churches inevitably condemned to extinction."

With that he gathered up his notes, brought the class to an end, and descended from the podium, declaiming in a voice loud enough for all to hear, "Saint Clement of Rome, Saint Ignatius of Antioch, Saint Irenaeus, Saint Augustine, Saint Gregory the Great, and all you holy Fathers of the Church, pray for us. Pray for us."

Just a few weeks after answering the aforementioned letter about Apostolic succession, I happened to be perusing the July 7 edition of the *New York Times*. On page 5 of the "Metro" section, my eye was caught by three large photographs of a Victorian-style church. According to the article accompanying the photographs, the edifice was located on West 57th Street in Manhattan and was undergoing extensive restoration. It had belonged, the article stated, to the Catholic Apostolic Church, which had ceased to exist officially in 1901, "when the last of its 'apostles' died."

Still, the article went on, a number of aging adherents had struggled to maintain some activity in their church for almost a century. Finally, though, with only a few congregations remaining, they decided to turn the building over to another Protestant denomination at no cost.

Later in the week, I had to travel to New York to visit a friend in a hospital very near West 57th Street, and I decided to go see the church that had gone out of existence for lack of "apostles."

Starting at Fifth Avenue and proceeding west on 57th Street, I stopped at stores and newsstands, holding up the page from the *Times* and inquiring about where the church in the three photographs might be. Finally, between Ninth and Tenth Avenues, at Number 417, I found it on my own. It was enshrouded from the cross on top to the sidewalk below with heavy blue canvas, under which one could hear workmen sandblasting the stone exterior.

I entered though a narrow side door. Slowly, my eyes grew accustomed to the gloom within. The pews had been removed, but the battered remains of two holy-water fonts and an ancient organ were still in place, as were an altar with a cracked marble tabernacle, several well-worn benches for the clergy, and a host of religious symbols on the walls and on the ceiling, most of them recalling the sacraments of Baptism and Eucharist.

I asked the man who seemed to be in charge of the restoration if I might roam through the building.

"Help yourself," he replied cheerily. "There's not much to see. We already discarded the statues and the pulpit."

He returned to his work, and I made my way into the sanctuary. It could have been designed for a Catholic Church, one with Apostolic succession. A limp chain hung from the ceiling to sustain a filigreed tabernacle lamp that lay broken on the floor below. Next to it were soot-covered vessels for incense, and next to them a pile of soiled stoles.

I entered the sacristy. In closets, the doors of which had been removed, there hung dozens of cassocks and albs, all wilted and coated with dust. Beside the closets were two finely carved vestment cases. On the drawers of each, titles were written in fading Spencerian script. One read "Only for Lenten Services," and another, "Feast Day Altar Cloths."

As I walked back into the body of the church, the man with whom I had spoken before told me how fortunate I was to have chosen to come this particular day.

"Tomorrow we won't be allowing any more visitors," he declared. "The next owner will be arriving soon with all new furniture."

He paused, mopped his brow, and turned back to me. "That's the first of the lot," he said, pointing to an imposing throne standing at the edge of the sanctuary with a bas-relief of a bishop's miter set into its high wooden back.

"What denomination is the new owner?" I inquired.

The man consulted a sheaf of papers on a clipboard attached to his thick leather belt. I was not surprised by his reply. It turned out to be a Christian communion that had eliminated the episcopacy in the religious conflicts of the 1500s, but, he claimed, had rather recently begun, especially in Germany and the United States, to refer to its ecclesiastical leadership as "bishops."

⌒

I walked out onto West 57th Street and, with a hint of a smile on my face, whispered to myself, "Saint Clement of Rome, Saint Ignatius of Antioch, Saint Irenaeus, Saint Augustine, Saint Gregory the Great, and all you holy saints of God, pray for us."

Somehow, I was sure that the wily professor who had taught me the meaning of Apostolic succession was smiling from his place in Heaven, and perhaps even joining his prayer to mine.

Bridgeport, December 1996

Wrappings

In the fall of 1958, I was assigned, fresh from the seminary, to Holy Name Cathedral Parish in Chicago as the ninth curate. Among my duties were working with another priest on what was then called "convert classes" and caring for Catholic patients on the sixth, seventh, and eighth floors of Wesley Memorial Hospital,[7] a renowned medical facility three blocks east of the cathedral.

The eighth floor of Wesley was dedicated to broken bones, especially broken hips, and the patients were mostly women who were well up in years.

⁀

On a cold day a few weeks before Christmas, I walked into one of the double rooms on the eighth floor of the hospital to greet the two ladies who were lodged there. My eyes were tearing from the frigid air outside, but my spirits were high, as spirits often are when one is coming in from the cold.

In my hand was a file card issued by the hospital concerning the lady in bed A. She was a Catholic of Slovak heritage who was evidently in a good deal of pain. There was no card for the lady in bed B, and from this I concluded that she was probably not Catholic.

[7] Renamed Northwestern Memorial Hospital in 1972.

"How are you ladies on this nice wintry day?" I asked in a less-than-successful attempt at cheeriness. The lady in bed A responded, "Not so good, Father. Not so good at all." The lady in bed B was silent.

"Is it the hip?" I asked the lady in bed A.

"It's the hip, Father," she replied, "and I broke it in my own kitchen. Mary, Mother of the Lord, I broke it in my own kitchen!"

I inquired if the lady in bed A would like to receive Holy Communion the next morning. She eagerly assured me that she would. Thus, I drew a heavy canvas curtain around her bed and heard her confession.

As the curtain was being pulled back in place, the lady in bed A presented me to the lady in bed B. "This is the Father, the priest," she said. "He will be bringing me Holy Communion tomorrow morning."

"I don't believe in priests," the lady in bed B responded. "And I don't believe in all of the Christmas decorations they have to put up in this hospital either. They are an offense to those of us who think differently, or perhaps I should say, to those of us who think."

The visit ended on that discordant note, and the next visit a week later was not much of an improvement. After I had indicated to the lady in bed A that I would be bringing her Communion again the next morning, the lady in bed B demanded, "Do you really believe, sir, in all of these Christmas goings-on? Or are you just taking advantage of simpleminded people?"

The lady in bed A squirmed but said nothing.

"Yes, I believe in all of it," I replied.

"And so do I," the lady in bed A added in a more than usually assertive tone.

"I even believe," I continued, "that the Almighty sent His only-begotten Son to become one of us to save us from our sins.

In fact, I believe that that selfsame Son of God was born of a young Jewish girl in Bethlehem almost two thousand years ago, that He spent His life doing good and preaching truth, and that He died on a Cross to make it possible for all of us to live forever in Heaven with Him and His Father."

"And with His Mother, too," the lady in bed A interjected in an ever more peremptory style.

The lady in bed B was clearly prepared for something of the sort.

"Well," she announced, "I will tell you what I believe. I believe that you people are foisting all of this on the rest of us, and that you are doing it in a thousand insidious ways. Christmas trees in the hospital corridors. Christmas carols over the hospital loudspeaker. Gifts wrapped in red and green on everyone's bed table. Red and green decorations everywhere. Everywhere red and green. It's brainwashing, that's what it is, and it ought to be stopped!"

In a small leather briefcase that I carried with me on hospital visits, I kept an assortment of rosaries, some paperbound prayer books specifically for the sick, and a copy or two of *A Catechism for Adults*, a publication that was regularly distributed to those who participated in the cathedral convert classes. Somewhat hesitantly, I laid a copy of the catechism on the table next to bed B, observing that it was a gift from me, that it was not wrapped in red and green, and that it should not, therefore, give offense. Stony silence greeted my gesture.

The lady in bed A, bolder now than ever, beckoned me to her side. "Give her a rosary like the one you gave me, Father," she whispered. "It won't be wrapped in red and green either."

I set a rosary in a blue plastic case on the table next to bed B and, with eyes cast down, took my leave.

The next week I came to make my visits on the eighth floor of Wesley Memorial Hospital with a measure of apprehension. There was, however, no reason to be concerned. The lady in bed A was still there, but the lady in bed B had gone home.

"My roommate asked to be remembered to you," the lady in bed A reported.

"I'll bet," I responded ruefully. "What did she do with my catechism?"

"Well, she said she did not think it was as 'adult' as its title promised," the lady in bed A responded. "Still, she and I discussed the fifteen decades of the Rosary on several occasions since you were here last. So I had a chance to tell her the story of each of the Mysteries in detail. She was really a very nice lady, and she even told me that she would read your catechism again and maybe sometime attend one of your classes at the cathedral."

"And, oh yes, Father," the lady in bed A continued. "She asked me to give you this."

With that she handed me a large white envelope on which was written in block letters: "For Father from the lady in bed B." I opened it. Inside was a black leatherette pocket agenda for the coming year fitted into a cardboard box that was wrapped in bright green tissue paper and topped with a red silk ribbon.

I thought I spied tears in the eyes of the lady in bed A, but I could not be sure. For there were tears in my own eyes, perhaps because of the cold outside, perhaps because of the red and green wrappings I held in my hands.

Bridgeport, January 1990

The Resurrection Cross

Fifth Avenue was unusually crowded for a Tuesday morning. I had taken a train to Grand Central Station and was making my way uptown for a meeting at Rockefeller Center. It was my plan to detour at 46th Street, where I hoped to find an artisan to repair my pectoral cross, the cross a bishop wears for Mass and other ceremonies.

The cross had been given to me by the seminarians of the Diocese of Bridgeport on the occasion of the tenth anniversary of my episcopal consecration. It is made of gilded silver and embossed with an image of the Lord seated on a throne, His right hand raised in blessing. Hidden in the back of it is a little chamber containing a tiny sliver from the True Cross, which Saint Helena, the mother of the first Christian emperor, had brought to Rome from the Holy Land in the fourth century A.D. As a result of frequent openings and closings in the course of my sermons, the cover of the chamber had come loose.

⁀

Forty-sixth Street seemed the logical place to find someone ready and able to repair the cross. As I turned off Fifth Avenue, peering into several stores selling gold and silver, I finally spied a likely candidate. He was seated in a booth close to the store window, meticulously repairing a gold pendant with the help of miniature binoculars attached to his eyeglasses. I entered the store with confidence.

The man gestured me toward a woman in the booth immediately next to his.

"Can I help you?" she inquired.

"Yes," I replied. "I need to have this little cover reattached."

The woman took my cross in her hands and examined it carefully. "How strange!" she exclaimed in a heavily accented voice. "Usually the Holy Lord on the cross is naked and suffering. Why is He this way on your cross?"

"Well," I began, somewhat taken aback, "this represents the Lord after He had risen from the dead and ascended into Heaven to be with His Father, and ours."

My response had a rather academic sound. Moving on, I struggled to do better.

"Both representations are proper," I explained. "The usual one reminds us that the Son of God died a terrible death on the Cross for our salvation, and this one emphasizes that He rose from the dead and awaits our resurrection with Him after we die."

"Lovely!" the woman exclaimed. "Lovely, lovely!"

With that, she turned to a man in the back of the booth whom I had not noticed. He was quite short, with thick eyeglasses and raven-black hair. The two of them spoke together at some length in a language I could not identify. All the while, they were passing the pectoral cross back and forth, at times studying the image of the Lord up close and at times admiring it at arm's length. Finally, the woman turned to me.

"We think your cross most beautiful," she declared. "We both believe in the Holy Lord and hope to live with Him in Heaven. We love the lesson of your cross."

The man interrupted and, in an English considerably less fluent than the woman's, announced, "Our friend in the first booth is being happy to repair your cross. We charge only for the work. No more. No more."

The friend in the first booth removed his miniature binoculars. Until then, he had not seemed to have been following our conversation. Suddenly, however, he came alive. "Let me see the Lord-in-Heaven cross," he pleaded. "Ah, most beautiful. I repair it. I, too, believe we will be raised up to Heaven with the Lord if we be good."

He hesitated slightly and added in a whisper, "Pray for me, priest."

The woman thrust into my hand a calling card on the back of which she had written, "Raised from Dead Cross. March 5. Pickup: 3 o'clock."

⁂

At 3:30, I was back at the store on 46th Street. The man with the thick eyeglasses and raven-black hair greeted me warmly and invited me to be seated on a stool in front of the lady's booth. "Our friend has repaired your cross," he reported. "He took it down the street to be specially polished. He wants it perfect."

"I want it perfect, too," echoed the woman who had given me the calling card. She was now seated in the rear of her booth. "I showed it to everyone who came into the store and even to the men in the back," she proclaimed. "I told them what this lovely cross means. I told them that the Holy Lord is raised from the dead. I told them He is in Heaven waiting for all of us. I told them everything."

While she was speaking, the man who had done the repair work entered the store. With a bit of drama, he set the pectoral cross on a piece of light-blue flannel that covered the counter. Under the fluorescent ceiling lamps, it sparkled as it had never sparkled before.

"See," he cried. "Beautiful! Perfect!"

Somewhat embarrassed, I paid the woman the meager amount that had been stipulated for the work. As she was making change, two men coming from the rear of the store passed behind me. The woman beckoned them over to her booth. Since they spoke in her language, I could not understand what was being said. Each of the men, however, inspected the cross with a reverence that I would not have anticipated; then one of them shook my hand lustily, while the other bowed repeatedly in my direction.

The woman beamed. "See," she said. "I told everyone. I told everyone everything."

⌐

The next morning, I chose the twenty-eighth chapter of the Gospel according to Saint Matthew for my meditation before Mass. The story is well known. Women came to the tomb of the Lord on Easter morning. They were greeted by an angel, who first informed them that the crucified Christ had been raised from the dead and then ordered them to proclaim the news far and wide. In the words of Saint Matthew, the women left the angel "quickly" and "ran" to tell the world what they had heard.

In the past, I might have wondered how it was that Providence had chosen women for the glorious task of first announcing the Resurrection. Now, of course, I fully understand. It all became crystal clear in a store on 46th Street in New York City one day in March.

Bridgeport, April 1996

Slowly, Thoughtfully, Joyfully

The newspapers had been writing about the ceremony for weeks. A Torah, that is, a scroll containing the first five books of the Old Testament, was to be installed in the new library of a local college of Hebrew studies. The year was 1967, and the Torah was alleged to be among the most ancient and elegant of such treasures to have been spirited out of Hungary since the dropping of the Iron Curtain over Eastern Europe.

The executive director of the Board of Rabbis invited me, as a representative of the Catholic community, to offer a prayer at the beginning of the ceremony. I agreed, with the understanding that he would help me choose some appropriate Hebrew words for the conclusion of my prayer and practice me in the proper pronunciation of them.

The ceremony went quite well. The mayor spoke, as did the lieutenant governor, several rabbis, and the president of the Council of Protestant Churches. Of the non-Jewish participants, however, only I had woven any Hebrew into what I had to say. Thus it was that, as I was about to leave, the director of the library rushed over to me and threw his arms around my shoulders.

"We are most grateful for your being here," he exclaimed, "and we were deeply touched by your speaking in the language of our people. Where did you learn your Hebrew?"

Not a little embarrassed, I replied that sometime I would let him in on my secret.

"No, no, no," he cried. "You must come to my home this very evening to explain it all."

His enthusiasm was such that I could not resist. I promised to arrive no later than half-past seven.

～

The home was on the sixth floor of a modern apartment complex. Still, when I entered it, I felt as though I were stepping into a charming Middle-Europe residence of a century before. The floors were covered with a collection of small Persian carpets. The windows were hung with heavy velvet drapes. The chairs and even some of the tables were adorned with silk throws from which flowed long, graceful tassels. And, everywhere throughout the two dimly lit parlors, neat stacks of books of all sizes were in evidence.

The director of the library handed me a delicately etched glass of what seemed to be a kind of port wine, gestured me into a huge leather chair, and raised his own glass with a smile of pleasure and welcome.

"My wife and her mother will be joining us in just a moment," he announced; and even as he spoke, they entered, each bearing a lacquered tray of cookies and little cakes.

"Now, tell me your secret," my host whispered in a mock conspiratorial tone. "Where did you, a Catholic priest, learn to speak Hebrew?"

"I don't speak Hebrew," I confessed. "A rabbi friend chose the verses that I recited in my prayer and drilled me on their pronunciation."

"So you never had a course in Hebrew?" he asked.

"Well, actually, I did," was my reply. "However, it was taught in Latin out of a German textbook in Italy, and I am afraid that my classmates and I did not learn very much."

"How much?" he insisted.

"We mastered some basic vocabulary. We could conjugate the regular verbs. We were able to struggle through uncomplicated Scripture passages with the aid of a dictionary. And ..." I hesitated but decided to go on. "And we memorized the opening chapter of the book of Genesis and a small part of the 'Servant Songs' of the prophet Isaiah. But that was all."

"That was quite a lot," he countered. "Do you still recall the opening chapter of the book of Genesis?"

"Perhaps," I replied, feeling a bit uneasy with his rather unyielding interrogation. "*Bereshith bara Elohim eth hashamyim we-eth haaertz*," I began, moving along quickly in the hope that sounds from many years before would filter back into my memory.

"Oh, no, Father," he interrupted. "Not that way! *Never* that way! When you speak the Word of God, you must do it slowly. You must do it thoughtfully. You must do it joyfully."

With that, he leaned back in his chair, closed his eyes, and almost as though he were in a trance repeated what I had started. "*Bereshith* ... In the beginning. In the very beginning. Before anything was. Before time. Before eternity. *Bara Elohim* ... our Lord. Our God. The Almighty One. The infinitely Good and Holy ... Created. Made from nothing. Gave reality where it had not been ..."

He went on in this way to the end of the chapter, saying the words in Hebrew, commenting on them in English, sipping his wine occasionally, and never allowing the atmosphere of prayerful delight that shone on his face to wane. And, all the while, his wife and mother-in-law sat back in their chairs, their eyes closed as well, savoring every word.

I felt as though I were witnessing a transport of thoroughly enjoyed meditation. Hence, I set my glass on the table next to me and folded my hands in prayer. The Word of God was swirling about the four of us. I had no doubt that the Spirit of God was at work as well.

Two years ago, when I came to Bridgeport, many books brought from Rome were in the basement of the retirement home on 34th Street, where I lived. I sent many to the seminary and discarded others. Two that I curiously kept were a Masoretic Text of the Old Testament and the German Hebrew Grammar. They stand in a bookcase in my office in my residence next to my collection of Bibles, biblical commentaries, and various books about Sacred Scripture. I am sure that I will never use them, but they are there to remind me about how to read the Word of God as taught by a wise, learned, and holy Rabbi — slowly, thoughtfully, and joyfully.

❧

All of this had long since slipped into the recesses of my memory, until I began reading the chapter in the new *Catechism of the Catholic Church*[8] that treats the first three of the Ten Commandments. The chapter is constructed as no other in the *Catechism*. It is a series of phrases from the Commandments as they appear in the twentieth chapter of the book of Exodus, with a commentary on each of them in an almost stream-of-consciousness style. The result is not so much a text of religious truths as a meditation on a powerful and moving portion of Holy Writ.

---

[8] The new *Catechism of the Catholic Church* was promulgated by Pope John Paul II in 1992 and published in English in 1994.

Thus, the words of the First Commandment, "You shall worship the Lord your God," lead the authors of the *Catechism* to discuss with delight the virtues of faith, hope, and charity. "Him only shall you serve" introduces a series of brief, thought-provoking reflections on such matters as adoration, prayer, and sacrifice. "You shall have no other gods before me" draws the reader into a graceful analysis of the wrongness of superstition and idolatry. And "You shall not make for yourself a graven image" introduces a defense of properly venerating representations of the Lord, His angels, and His saints.

A similar approach is adopted in treating the Second Commandment. The individual phrases from Exodus are set forth in bold print, and a variety of loosely connected considerations flow from each. The reader, for instance, is invited to revere the name of the Lord, to seek in it "a sense of the sacred," to avoid blasphemy and false oaths, and to understand the evil of perjury.

Finally, the prohibition against taking God's holy name "in vain" curiously and unexpectedly provokes an investigation into the wisdom of choosing the name of a saint for one who is to be baptized, a saint "who has lived a life of exemplary fidelity to the Lord."

The treatment of the Third Commandment, at the conclusion of the chapter, is likewise structured to begin with words from Exodus and proceed to a reflective examination of such diverse subjects as the Sabbath of the Old Testament, the Lord's Day of the New Testament, the Eucharist, parishes, liturgical participation, and the spiritual significance of resting from work at sacred times. Perhaps just the following two excerpts from this final section of the chapter will give some insight into the prayerful charm of the whole:

Jesus rose from the dead "on the first day of the week."[9] Because it is the "first day," the day of Christ's Resurrection recalls the first creation. Because it is the "eighth day" following the Sabbath,[10] it symbolizes the new creation ushered in by Christ's Resurrection. For Christians it has become the first of all days, the first of all feasts, the Lord's Day—Sunday....

Those Christians who have leisure should be mindful of their brethren who have the same needs and the same rights, yet cannot rest from work because of poverty and misery. Sunday is traditionally consecrated by Christian piety to good works and humble service of the sick, the infirm, and the elderly. Christians will also sanctify Sunday by devoting time and care to their families and relatives, often difficult to do on other days of the week. Sunday is a time for reflection, silence, cultivation of the mind, and meditation which furthers the growth of the interior life. (CCC 2174, 2186)

A careful reading of the new *Catechism* is a splendid act of piety. It deepens our knowledge of the Faith, and it strengthens our commitment to a life of virtue. The chapter on the first three Commandments, however, goes a step further. For, in addition to informing us about what has been revealed and spurring us on to holier lives, it provides, as well, a lesson on how to read the Word of God.

---

[9] Cf. Matt. 28:1; Mark 16:2; Luke 24:1; John 20:1.
[10] Cf. Mark 16:1; Matt. 28:1.

"Pick up your Bible," the authors of the *Catechism* are saying, "open to a passage that inspires, and read it in the way we have read the text of the first three Commandments in the book of Exodus. Stop at the end of each phrase. Think about what it means. Comment on it in your own words. Massage it. Savor it. Cherish it. And do not go on until you have heard—and spoken—all that it has to say to you at this moment in your life. Soon, you will find the reading of Sacred Scripture to be not just a recitation of lovely words but rather a prayer, a meditation, a contemplation, a marvelous and joyous 'connecting' with your God."

All of this I had been told, in effect, many years before in the home of a learned holy man. I was mouthing a segment of Scripture, and he insisted that I pray it. "Not that way! *Never* that way!" he declared. "When you speak the Word of God, you must do it slowly. You must do it thoughtfully. You must do it joyfully."

It was a lesson that I needed to hear again; and I heard it a second time most tellingly from another learned and holy source—the *Catechism of the Catholic Church*.

Bridgeport, March 1995

"An Advent Catholic"

In my first months as a priest in the cathedral parish of the Archdiocese of Chicago, I had three principal duties. The first was to care for the patients on three floors of a local hospital. The second was to assist in "inquiry classes" for persons interested in becoming Catholic. And the third was to take a "census" of all individuals and families in four large apartment buildings a short distance from the cathedral rectory.

In mid-October of that first year of my priesthood, I knocked one morning at the apartment door of a man who was well known to the priests of the cathedral but unknown to me. He was a widower, and I was therefore surprised when a woman opened the door. She informed me that the man I had come to see was not feeling well, and she suggested that I come back some other time. (I will call her Valerie, and I will call him Charlie, although these were not their real names.)

From the bedroom, a voice was heard. "Who is that, Valerie?" it thundered.

"A priest," she answered.

"Bring him in, bring him in," the voice commanded. And in I went.

"Well, Father, what brings you here on this lovely day in autumn?" Charlie asked.

"I am making my regular parish census calls," I replied. "If you're not up to it, I can come back some other time."

"No, sit down," Charlie responded. "I am glad to see you. Of late, I have been a bit under the weather. So I have Valerie from the hospital staying with me from nine in the morning until nine at night, and she has agreed to come on weekends, too. The doctor is having tests done, and I am hoping for the best. With Valerie's care and your prayers, I'm sure all will be well."

I fidgeted a bit in my chair, not knowing what to say or do. It seemed out of place to pull out my census card and start asking questions.

Charlie intuited my discomfiture and out of nowhere asked me, "What are you going to do for Advent, Father?"

Somewhat caught off guard, I began to fumble for an answer when Valerie interrupted to ask what *Advent* means. She noted that, although she was not a Catholic, she was "a believing Christian."

Charlie broke into a long explanation of Advent, the details of which took me by surprise. He knew that there were four Sundays in Advent. He knew that the priest at Mass wore purple vestments on three of the Sundays and rose vestments on a fourth, which, he observed, "is actually the third of the four." He even knew that *Advent* is from the Latin word for "coming" and has to do not only with the coming of the Lord in Bethlehem, but also with His coming again at the end of time.

"And so, Father, what are you going to do for Advent?" he repeated.

"Well," I stuttered, "in the seminary the spiritual director told us that we should read the four Gospels during Advent and recommended that we read a passage from one of them each day for five minutes, and then meditate on what we have read for ten minutes. I'm going to do that."

The answer was accurate, as far as the suggestion of the spiritual director was concerned, but not as regards my decision. The decision was taken right there on the spot, so as to make the best of a rather awkward situation.

"Great!" Charlie cried. "The next time you come to see this sick old man, bring me a book with the four Gospels in it from the cathedral bookstore. I'll follow the program laid out by your spiritual director. What is it again?"

Like a medical doctor who had just written a prescription and was telling his patient how to use the recommended medicine, I repeated the formula: "Read from the Gospels each day for five minutes and meditate on what you read for ten minutes." (I was tempted to add, "And call me in the morning," but decided that joking might be out of place.)

"Sounds good," Charlie proclaimed. "If you could come to see me again on Sunday afternoon, it would be great. I think I am going to be laid up for quite a while. And another thing," he went on, "maybe you could bring me Communion when you bring me the book of the Gospels. It will be the First Sunday of Advent, won't it?"

I acknowledged that it would, gave him my blessing, and went on my way.

⁀

A few days later, I purchased two copies of a book containing just the four Gospels. They were sturdy, bound in imitation leather, and rather inexpensive. Hence, I bought one also for myself.

On the First Sunday of Advent, I arrived at Charlie's apartment with the two books in a bag from the bookstore, set the bag on a table next to his bed, and arranged the crucifix, candles, and such. Unfortunately, when Charlie reached for the bag, it fell to the floor and the two books slipped out.

"Look, Valerie," Charlie announced with delight. "Father got you a book, too. We will do Advent together." Valerie thanked me with a certain hesitation in her voice, and I accepted her expression of gratitude as though I deserved it.

"Five minutes reading the Gospels each day, and ten minutes thinking about it: Is that the ticket, Father?" Charlie asked.

"Yes, that's it exactly," I agreed with the air of a seasoned practitioner of the medical profession and gave him Communion.

The next Sunday, when I arrived with the Eucharist, I was struck by how poorly Charlie looked. The following Sunday, when I knocked at the door, Valerie appeared, pushed me out into the hallway, and told me that Charlie did not have long to live. "He's full of cancer," she said.

When we moved into Charlie's room, Valerie put a smile on her face and reported that they were doing their "five minutes of reading and ten minutes of thinking" every day, adding that Charlie had been considering changing the formula to "ten minutes of reading and fifteen minutes of thinking."

I was about to say that that might be too much but thought better of it. Sometimes the patient knows more than the doctor, I told myself.

⁓

The Fourth and last Sunday of Advent found Charlie in the hospital. I went to see him after the last Mass at the cathedral. His book of the Gospels was open on the bed, and Valerie's was open on her lap. She told me that the end was near. I absolved him, anointed him, gave him Communion, and concluded with the Apostolic Blessing at the Hour of Death.

"An Advent Catholic"

Three days later, I saw my name on the bulletin board of the cathedral sacristy as deacon for Charlie's funeral Mass, which was to have the rector of the cathedral as celebrant. (In those days, the celebrant was regularly accompanied at funeral Masses by priests fulfilling the roles of deacon and subdeacon.) The rector, in his sermon, stated that he was sure that Charlie was well prepared to go to His Lord, and his statement meant a great deal to me. Deep down, I knew how truly and thoroughly prepared he was.

At Eastertime, I saw Valerie after Mass in the cathedral. She had joined its most recent inquiry class, she told me, and become a Catholic. She confided to me how much she had come to admire Charlie during their Advent together.

"Reading the Gospels every day was something I will never forget," she said. "I am going to do it every Advent for as long as the Lord keeps me on this planet."

With that, she gave me a kiss on the cheek and whispered, "That's from an Advent Catholic."

For over half a century, whenever anyone asks me what to do for Advent, I always have a ready answer. In the interest of full disclosure, perhaps I should confess that it is also my "prescription" for Lent.

New York, December 2008

"Tradition"

The bus that moves uptown on First Avenue in Manhattan is often half empty when it stops at 34th Street to pick up passengers at eight o'clock in the morning. Hence, when I boarded it to go to the Catholic Center of the Archdiocese on 55th Street, where I worked, I usually found myself a window seat in which I could quietly read my Breviary during the twenty-minute journey.

Frequently, a religious Sister who worked with me in the Archdiocesan Education Office was on the same bus, reading her Breviary as well. She was a Sister of Charity who wore the traditional garb: a long habit and the classic bonnet of Mother Seton.

We would regularly get off the bus together at 54th Street and cross over to the Catholic Center, chatting more often than not about Catholic schools, "one of the Church's most precious treasures," as Sister liked to describe them.

~

One morning, early in the spring of 1988, I remained on the bus until 57th Street in order to walk over to the Chase Bank on Third Avenue to transact some personal business. The passenger who exited the bus behind me tapped me on the shoulder as I stepped off the curb. He was a man of perhaps thirty years of age, short, portly, and blessed with a bright, flashing smile.

"I like to be on the bus with the nun and you, Padre," he announced. "In this crazy town, it's nice to be with people reading Bibles for everyone to see."

I was somewhat taken aback by his warmth and familiarity. "I will tell Sister what you said, and she will be delighted," I replied. And then, always the schoolteacher, I added, "What we read on the bus are not exactly Bibles. They are Breviaries, which contain passages from the Bible, but also sermons and stories from Tradition."

My fellow traveler grinned broadly and sang the word *Tradition* to the tune of a song by that name from the Broadway musical *Fiddler on the Roof*.

"Where are you headed, Padre?" he inquired.

"Over to Third Avenue," I responded.

"I'm going in that direction too," he reported. And as we crossed First Avenue, he kept on half singing the word *Tradition* and laughing heartily after each rendition.

"What's this 'Tradition' in your prayer book?" he asked when we were safely on our way along 57th Street.

"It's the living teaching of the Church from the time of the Apostles until now," I observed a bit pedantically. And, with that, I handed him my briefcase so that I could open my Breviary and show him some "Tradition."

The first example was from a sermon of Pope Saint Leo the Great; the second, from a chapter of the *Catechism of Saint John Chrysostom*; and the third, from a section on the *Constitution on the Church in the Modern World* of the Second Vatican Council.

"That's Tradition," I proclaimed, smiling and singing the word as well as I could.

We crossed Second Avenue, and my friend took hold of my arm. The joviality had drained out of his face.

"I'm a Catholic," he whispered, looking down at his shoes, "but I don't know anything about my Faith. I went to public schools and just a few catechism classes before First Holy Communion and ..." His voice trailed off. "And I don't have a clue about the Church I think I love," he added mournfully.

There were a few moments of silence. I opened my briefcase, pulled out a pad, and invited him to write down his name, address, and telephone number. He kept his eyes riveted on the ground, and somehow I sensed that they were being blurred by tears welling up right there on 57th Street a few minutes before nine in the morning.

"I am going to send you some reading material, and put you in contact with the priests of your parish," I explained. "They will know all about the Bible and ..."

I was tempted to sing *Tradition*, but simply spoke it. The mood had changed. This was no time for levity.

By ten o'clock, I was in my office wading through the mail. Curiously, in one large envelope I found two Bibles and a book entitled *John Paul II in America*, all from the publishing house of the Daughters of Saint Paul. The Bibles were paperbound and illustrated with handsome pen-and-ink drawings. The book was a collection of the forty-eight sermons and addresses that the Holy Father had delivered in September 1987, during his pastoral visit to the United States.

I placed the book and one of the Bibles in a tufted mailing envelope, along with a note. "Here is the Word of God plus some powerful 'Tradition,'" I wrote on a card that I attached, adding,

"I will ask one of the priests in your parish to be in touch with you soon."

Three weeks or so passed, and I had not seen my new friend on the First Avenue bus or heard that he had received the books I sent him. Then, one morning, I received in my office a large business envelope and found inside two Sunday bulletins from a Long Island parish. A "From the desk of" note was slipped into one of the bulletins.

"We have moved to Long Island," it read, "and I am going to Mass at my new parish, as you can see from the attached. I read the 'Tradition' first and loved it. (The Pope's talk in San Antonio about our needing forgiveness from the Lord is great.) And, oh yes, my parish priest tells me that you are a bishop. Don't worry—I didn't tell him that you aren't much of a singer. Have you learned to sing the hit song from *Fiddler on the Roof* yet?"

I laid the bulletin and the note on my desk and, with immense satisfaction—and perhaps limited musicality—hummed "Tradition."

Bridgeport, April 1992

Repentances

For twenty years, the painting hung over a sideboard in the dining room of a rectory on Leeson Street in Dublin. A brass plate attached to the bottom of its ornate frame announced that it was the work of Gerrit van Honthorst, a student of one of the master painters of the Italian Renaissance, Michelangelo Merisi da Caravaggio, commonly known simply as Caravaggio.

In the summer of 1990, the rectory was to undergo a long-deferred redecorating. Thus, the painting was taken down, and a decision had to be made as to whether it should be kept. It was drab, badly in need of cleaning, and a bit too large for the space over the sideboard. Perhaps the best course, the priests felt, would be to try to find a buyer.

Accordingly, the pastor telephoned a friend who was also the director of the National Gallery of Ireland to seek his advice about selling the painting. The friend came to see it a few days later, bringing with him a young Italian by the name of Sergio Benedetti, who had been hired some months before to supervise the cleaning and restoring of the Renaissance works in the gallery's collection.

Benedetti was shocked when he entered the rectory dining room. From the moment he saw the painting, which was on the floor leaning up against a chair, he sensed that he was in the presence of a masterpiece. It depicted Judas with his hands stretched toward the Lord in the midst of three helmeted guards and two confused Apostles.

"Could this be the long-lost *Taking of Christ* by Caravaggio?" Benedetti asked himself as his heart began to pound. He would keep calm. He would not reveal his suspicions. He would only suggest that the painting be sent to the gallery workshop for an inspection and perhaps a cleaning as well.

≈

The inspection did not take long, since the signs of the master's hand were marvelously clear. For centuries, art connoisseurs had known that the thrifty Caravaggio used to stretch his canvases himself rather than have them professionally prepared, and the canvas in the gallery workshop was a typical example of his ineptness in this regard.

Moreover, black outlines of the various subjects in the painting could be seen through the colors that were intended to cover them. This too was compelling evidence of a Caravaggio original. For, unlike virtually all the Italian artists of his time, Caravaggio refused to make preliminary drawings of his paintings. Instead, he sketched the individual figures one by one on his canvases with broad strokes of black undercoat, confident that a balanced composition would be achieved as the work progressed.

What, however, removed all doubt about the provenance of the painting was something that art experts have come to call *pentimenti*, that is, repaintings of sections of a canvas after the pigments have dried in order to make corrections and improvements.

Recognizing that changes are needed and seeing to them, these experts insist, belong exclusively to those who create original works. "A copyist only repeats, while a master willingly repents," they love to proclaim. And the painting that hung for years in the rectory on Leeson Street was a mass of these *pentimenti*, or, if you prefer, these "repentances."

Two of the most prominent were to be found on the ear of Judas and in the shadowing on the face of the Lord. Looking closely, one could easily see that the artist had repainted the betrayer's ear at least three times, in each instance making it smaller. Likewise, the shadow that Judas's head casts on the brow and cheek of Christ had obviously been worked over and over again; and with each reworking it became more and more clear that Judas was not leaning into the Lord to embrace Him, but rather struggling to pull away from Him.

~

When I read all of this, first in a local newspaper, and then in a national newsmagazine, I was thoroughly captivated by the story. It was, I believed, a natural jumping-off point for a sermon or homily on sin and repentance, and I used it with shameless frequency.

The great Caravaggio had a lesson for us all, I would declare. Judas had stopped listening to the Lord. He was attending, instead, to the criticisms and challenges of the worldly wise who could not understand, for example, the "waste" of precious perfume by the penitent Magdalene as she knelt at the feet of her Lord. The ear of the errant Apostle needed, therefore, to be made ever smaller. For as long as we stay attuned to the voice of the Savior in prayer, in the Scriptures, and in the teachings of the Church, Caravaggio is telling us, betrayal is unlikely. When, however, we stop listening, he continues, betrayal becomes all but inevitable.

Similarly, I would go on, the tragedy of Judas according to Caravaggio was not his kiss. It was rather his unwillingness after the kiss to seek forgiveness. It was not his leaning into the Son of God to betray Him that was his downfall. It was, rather, his pulling away from that same Son of God, refusing to seek forgiveness.

And the artist kept correcting and "repenting" until these two messages were driven home with crystalline clarity. Never stop struggling to hear the voice of the Lord, and your reasons to repent will be few, he is telling us. And when you need to repent, he adds, do not pull away in shame or fear. Rather, lean into your God, grab hold of Him, and with unwavering trust implore His absolution.

⁐

On June 20, 1997, the Metropolitan Museum of Art in New York City announced that it had just acquired what is thought to be the last painting of Caravaggio. It is entitled *The Denial of Peter* and is said to have been purchased from a private collector in Switzerland for between thirty and forty million dollars.

After having completed a number of errands on a hot July day in Manhattan, I made my way to see the new acquisition. As I entered Gallery 30, on the second floor, I had no trouble whatever finding it. For clustered about the elegantly framed canvas were five young German men and three French-Canadian ladies "of a certain age," and there was no one else in the mammoth room inspecting any of the other Renaissance masterpieces.

One of the Germans, an uncommonly tall fellow in lederhosen, stepped aside to permit me to draw closer to the painting. "*Wunderbar!*" he exclaimed in a tone that seemed to call for an expression of agreement on my part.

"*Jawohl,*" I answered rather meekly, hoping that the narrow limits of my German would not be tried in an ensuing conversation.

Repentances

The eldest of the French-Canadian ladies came to my rescue.

"*Mon Père,*" she inquired, "*avez-vous rémarque les 'pénitences'?*" (Have you noticed the "repentances"?) She moved to the left so that I might better observe the artist's corrections in the light reflecting off the highly varnished surface of the painting.

"*Oui,*" I replied, "*je les vois.*" (Yes, I see them.) And see them I did, in several evident corrections in the tormented eyes and pathetically twisted hands of the penitent Prince of the Apostles.

"*Oui,*" I repeated with feeling, "*je les vois.*"

∽

As the tourists continued to admire the Caravaggio, I quietly took my leave, for I was anxious to catch an early train back to Fairfield County.

Before going to Grand Central Station, however, I took a bus downtown to a church where I regularly go to confession. There I planned, first, to listen for a time to the Lord in prayer and then, in repentance, to lean into Him to beg forgiveness for my betrayals.

Bridgeport, September 1997

"Shocked"

On the weekend of November 25 and 26, one of our New York newspapers ran an article entitled, "Pope Shocks Theologians by Suggesting He May Be Fallible." The occasion of the "shock" was a statement by Pope Benedict XVI that a book about the life of Christ that he was writing would not entail the exercise of his infallible teaching authority. It would be religious. It would express his views about matters spiritual. It would be the result of years of study and prayers. But infallible it would not be.

One theological "expert" quoted in the newspaper article was sure that nothing of this sort had ever happened before. Another opined that Pope John Paul II would never have approved his successor's statement. And a third alleged that, by his declaration, Pope Benedict XVI was somehow "seeking to have his cake and eat it, too."

⌒

What theological training any of these "experts" might have had the newspaper does not reveal. This much, however, should be clear to any Catholic with even the most elementary catechetical formation: The "experts" quoted in the article knew nothing about papal infallibility.

Actually, the doctrine of papal infallibility is not at all complicated. If a Pope asserts that it will rain tomorrow, he may be right; but his assertion would not be, and could not be, infallible. Similarly, if a Pope were to insist that the Roman soccer team known as Roma is superior to the Roman soccer team known as Lazio, he may be right; but again, that upon which he insisted would not be, and could not be, infallible.

For, from the crystal-clear statements of two ecumenical councils (Vatican Council I, session 4, chapter 4; and Vatican Council II, Dogmatic Constitution on the Church, number 25) and numerous authoritative declarations of the Popes, we understand that the following conditions must be fulfilled for the exercise of papal infallibility:

1. The Holy Father must be acting in virtue of his authority as the supreme shepherd and teacher of the Church. It is not enough that he is saying what he holds to be true as an ordained clergyman or even a bishop. He must be speaking as the Roman Pontiff who uniquely succeeds in the office of Saint Peter, the Prince of the Apostles and the Bishop of Rome.

2. The Holy Father must be addressing the entire Church. Thus, a retreat for a group of religious, a homily at a parish Mass, or even a book about the spiritual life would not entail infallibility. All would be listened to or read with attention and respect, of course. Still, to be infallible teaching, they must be clearly intended for all the faithful, without exception.

3. Finally, the Holy Father must be treating matters of faith (what we believe) or morals (how we are expected by our God to act). Statements about other issues are

outside the parameters of infallible teaching. The forecast about the weather and the opinion about the soccer teams are obvious examples. Divine assistance protecting the Successor of Saint Peter from error in teaching is limited to the realm of what we believe and what the law of God requires of us. Declarations about other matters may be expressions of great insight and wisdom, but they have nothing to do with infallibility.

Is the book on the life of Christ to be authored by Pope Benedict XVI,[11] who has meditated on that life for years and plumbed the depths of its meaning with intense study, an expression of papal infallibility? Not at all. And this is clear not only because the Holy Father in question has stated that it is not such an expression, but also because it does not fulfill the conditions specified above. It is not an exercise of the supreme teaching authority of the Supreme Teacher in the Church because that Supreme Teacher has not willed to make it so. It is not addressed to all of the faithful, although all who wish to read it and be inspired by it are most welcome to do so. And it is not a pronouncement as to what we must believe or what before our God we must do.

Indeed, if someone were to suggest it is infallible, that would be "shocking."

⁀

One of the great blessings of my life is the theological education that I was given in Rome on my way to the priesthood. As a

---

[11] *Jesus of Nazareth*, the first of three volumes on the life and teachings of Jesus Christ written by Pope Benedict XVI, was published in 2007.

seminarian, I lived, prayed, and was prepared for pastoral service in a college near the Vatican, the Pontifical North American College, and took the bulk of my classes at a university on the other side of town, the Pontifical Gregorian University.

At the Gregorian, literally hundreds of us sat together in huge classrooms called aulas, hearing some of the most noted theologians of the day (the early 1950s). In the mornings we listened to the lectures and in the afternoon returned to our colleges, where tutors or, as we said in those days, Repetitors, reviewed and drilled what we had heard.

The professor who taught the tract on the Church to my classmates and the other seminarians in the aula, who came from across the world, was Reverend Timotheus Zapelena, S.J. He was recognized as an expert regarding papal infallibility, and thus his lectures were regularly attended also by guests who sat in a balcony high above our heads.

In great detail, Father Zapelena recounted the history of the First Vatican Council, during which, in July 1870, the doctrine of papal infallibility was declared to be a teaching of the Church to be held by all who count themselves followers of Jesus Christ. He analyzed each of the conditions for the exercise of the papal prerogative mentioned above and then explained each of the texts from the New Testament that sustained the doctrine. Among these were the section from the Gospel of Saint Matthew in which Peter is named the rock upon which the Church is built, is given the keys of the kingdom of Heaven, and is authorized to bind and loose on earth what will be bound and loosed in Heaven; and the section from the Gospel of Saint John in which Peter is appointed to feed the lambs and sheep of the Lord.

However, Father Zapelena became most animated when treating a text that is less familiar to most Catholics, but was clearly of great power in the mind of our distinguished professor: a text from the Gospel of Saint Luke (22:24-32).

⤳

Even now I can see the old Spanish Jesuit in my mind's eye. His face is covered with disappointment as he reports that the Apostles were arguing among themselves as to which of them was "the greatest." He takes off his *birettum* (a hat with three flaps on top that the clergy wore in that era) and, with head bent and great solemnity, recites the words of the Lord reminding the Apostles that they are not be seeking to be the "greatest" but, rather, to be "servants," as He was.

Finally, replacing the *birettum*, he straightens up and virtually shouts into the rafters of the immense aula in which we are assembled: "Simon, Simon, take heed. Satan has given leave to sift all of you like wheat. But I have prayed for you, Simon, that your faith might not fail. And when you are restored [that is, when you have repented from denying me, as I know you will], strengthen your brothers."

"This is what papal infallibility is all about," our professor first whispers and next repeats in a trembling voice. "The Lord Himself has prayed that the faith of Peter, and all of the Peters of all times, will never fail; and it never has and never will." He hesitates a moment, and continues, "Moreover, that same Lord has ordered Peter, and all the Peters of all times, to strengthen or, as one translation puts it particularly well, to 'make firm' the faith of all of us. That, too, is what papal infallibility is all about, and what a splendid gift it is to the Church and to each and every one of us."

With that, Father Zapelena removes his *birettum*, bows from the waist, slowly descends the steps of the podium from which he was speaking, and takes his leave amid the applause of both students and visitors. You know that he has thoroughly enjoyed his lecture and all the drama and devotion he has put into it, and you know, too, that no one who has heard him on the subject of papal infallibility will ever forget the experience.

~

Over the past fifty-two years, I have been blessed to see with my own eyes and hear with my own ears six Successors of Saint Peter. Never have I been in the presence of any of them without recalling the lecture of Father Zapelena on the text from the Gospel of Saint Luke that he evidently loved so much. When the Holy Father comes into view, I am reminded that the Lord has prayed that his faith will never fail and has, moreover, ordered him, as Successor of Saint Peter, to strengthen my faith and that of the entire Church as well.

What an immense responsibility, and what a marvelous blessing for all of us!

At the same time, I am also reminded that, while every Pope is free to exercise the gift of papal infallibility when he judges this right and necessary, such an exercise is rare indeed. In the ordinary course of events, the Successors of Saint Peter teach the truths of revelation as they know them and revere them, without invoking infallible teaching authority. And to all such noninfallible teaching we followers of the Divine Savior respond with the greatest of interest and the deepest of respect, as we will when Pope Benedict XVI publishes his life of Christ and "has his cake and eats it, too."

New York, December 2006

Holy Men and Women

"What made him the splendid disciple of the Lord that he was?" my director demanded. "I will tell you. Not the parishes, not the schools, not the catechisms, not the cathedral or the seminary. No, it was rather a quality of soul that must distinguish every priest, indeed, every follower of Jesus Christ. And that quality is kindness — the willingness to feel the pain of others, to care for others, even to sacrifice oneself for others."

A Knock at the Door

The papal-audience hall was filled to capacity. It was Wednesday, July 2, 2008. I had come to Rome with my priest-secretary to participate in meetings on Thursday and Friday with two Vatican finance committees on which I serve. We arrived on Tuesday so as to be able to attend the regular Wednesday audience, an experience that never fails to deepen faith and inspire hope.

In the course of the audience, the Holy Father, Pope Benedict XVI, took the occasion to deliver an unusually long address in which he explained that throughout the coming year, the so-called Pauline Year,[12] the theme of his audience addresses would be the life and teachings of Saint Paul, "a figure in our history," he said, "who was totally dedicated to Christ and His Church."

While listening to the Holy Father, I decided to follow his example by making the Apostle of the Gentiles the focus of my *Catholic New York* articles over the next twelve months. However, I further decided that the first of these articles would not be about the earliest years of Paul's life, as might be expected, but rather about an event that occurred toward the end of it. For I wanted to persuade my readers right from the start that

---

[12] Pope Benedict XVI proclaimed a special Jubilee Year from June 28, 2008, to June 29, 2009, to mark the approximately two thousandth anniversary of Saint Paul's birth.

the Apostle's story is not all *Sturm und Drang*, censures and controversies, struggles and heroics. I was anxious to present him in what I considered a more fair and accurate light, making it clear that the zealous "athlete of Christ" who "fought the good fight" was also a kind and compassionate follower of the "meek and humble" Savior.

To be sure that I had clearly in mind all the facts of the event I wished to narrate, on Saturday morning, my priest-secretary and I made our way to the place where the tale I wanted to tell actually unfolded more than nineteen hundred years ago.

≈

Unless you know the Eternal City very well indeed, you will not easily find the Church of San Paolo alla Regola, the site of my story. It is an unpretentious edifice, much in need of repair, located in a distressed neighborhood of Rome that is hardly ever visited by tourists. It stands two blocks away from where the ancient Ponte Sisto (Bridge of Sixtus) crosses the Tiber.

The words *alla Regola* in its title are meant to indicate that the church is situated in the area of Rome where the sand from the Tiber is deposited when the river overflows its banks. (*Regola* comes from the word for "sand" in a dialect that is still spoken in a surprising number of Roman households even today.)

My first visit to San Paolo alla Regola was made over fifty years ago. I was with a group of twelve fellow seminarians on one of the "Roman walks" we were required to take to churches, museums, and such three afternoons a week.

Upon entering the building, we were greeted by an elderly priest of the Third Order of Saint Francis who identified himself as the pastor and proved to be a most warm and cordial pastor at that. We began to walk around the church while our student prefect read a description of it from a classic guidebook authored by an Anglican clergyman who became a Catholic toward the end of the 1800s, Augustus J. B. Hare.

The pastor interrupted the reading and beckoned us toward a set of doors to the right of the sanctuary. He stood there with drama in his eyes and, when he had gained the attention of us all, knocked on one of the doors.

In due course he whispered, "Come in," trying to give the impression that the voice had come from within. He opened the door in a gingerly fashion and led us into a vast room in which there was nothing to be seen apart from a large mosaic on the back wall depicting Saint Paul chained to two soldiers and a pair of marble plaques over the doors inscribed with citations from the Second Epistle of Paul to Timothy (2:9) and the Acts of the Apostles (28:20).

"In an apartment here," the pastor announced, "the Apostle lived for three years during his first imprisonment in Rome. Because he was a Roman citizen and the charges against him were not at all convincing, he escaped being put into prison. Still, he was not free to leave his residence unless chained to two Praetorian guards. His situation was identified in Roman law as *Custodia libera*, which was a form of what we might call house arrest.

"One afternoon," our narrator continued, "there came a knock at Paul's door. The visitor was a Roman slave in a state of physical and emotional exhaustion. His name was Onesimus, and when the guards left the room at Paul's request, the slave confessed that he had stolen valuable items from his master, a certain Philemon who resided in Colossae, and that he had fled in panic when his crime was discovered. Now all that remained for him, he sobbed, was a branding on the forehead with the letter *F* for 'fugitive' and hard labor in horrific tin mines, where he would certainly die in a matter of weeks.

"Paul listened attentively to what the slave had to say," the pastor went on, "and after mulling over several courses of action, sat down and wrote a letter in favor of Onesimus to Philemon, whom he had brought into the Christian Faith some years earlier in Colossae."

⁓

"Never was there a more wonderful letter," the white-haired Franciscan proclaimed with a good deal of emotion in his voice. "Read it over and over. It is only twenty-five verses long. Still, if you meditate it and come to love it, it will work wonders for your spiritual life. Never, when someone comes knocking at your door for help, will you fail to open up and lend a willing hand.

"Paul," the pastor observed, "put himself in real peril when he chose to help Onesimus. The guards might have been eavesdropping and might have thought it their duty to report the slave's confession to their superiors. The Apostle, however, did not allow any of this to deter him from coming to the aid of another in need. Rather, he composed a brief but brilliant plea to Philemon to forgive Onesimus and gave it to a friend to deliver to Colossae with all possible speed. This is the Paul that one might easily miss when reading and following his adventures in the Acts of the Apostles, a compassionate, loving human being who felt the fear and hurt of a slave and, counting not the cost, risked his life and freedom to help him.

"You young men," the pastor concluded, "must never forget your visit to San Paolo alla Regola, and when you are priests, you must never hesitate to open your door and your heart to those who are hurting and in need. Be like Paul—compassionate, caring, and concerned for all who are frightened and suffering, without exception, without distinction."

⁀

The epistle to Philemon, which the pastor praised so warmly, is a triumph of Christian charity and a masterpiece of diplomacy, literary style, and even humor.

It opens with a salutation to Philemon and his family from "Paul, a prisoner for Christ Jesus." This is followed by a fine example of what the Greek and Roman rhetoricians called *captatio benevolentiae*, which in simplest terms is a strategy to win the sympathy of someone to whom a petition is being addressed by extolling his character or noble works.

Clearly this is what Paul had in mind when he wrote to Philemon in these words: "I give thanks to my God for you. I know the faith that you have in the Lord Jesus, and I know that the hearts of God's people are refreshed by you, my dear brother."

The Apostle then addresses his central concern. He observes that he should probably *order* Philemon to do what he will be asking of him, given his plight as a prisoner, his advanced years, and his having instructed Philemon in the precious truths of the Gospel. (A diplomat is clearly at work here.) He had with him, he states, the slave, Onesimus, whom he would like to keep for himself but whom he has decided to send back to Philemon so that the master might graciously embrace him and generously forgive and forget his misbehavior. (More diplomacy!)

Realizing, however, that he may be getting a bit heavy-handed, the Apostle introduces into his letter a clever play on words. In Greek, he reminds Philemon, *Onesimus* means "useful." Should Philemon do as Paul asks, the slave will certainly become

marvelously useful, the Apostle observes. For he will have provided both his master in Colossae and his advocate in Rome
with splendid opportunities to act with Christlike compassion.
And what could be more "useful" than that?

The appeal having been made, the Apostle immediately raises
the ante. When Onesimus returns to Colossae, he tells Philemon,
he is to be considered "no longer as a slave, but as a beloved
brother." For after their conversation, the Apostle reveals, he
instructed and baptized Onesimus and thus became his "father
in the Lord."

Finally, to leave Philemon completely disarmed, the Apostle
concludes his request with an offer he knows Philemon will
not take up. If Onesimus has caused Philemon any financial
loss, the Apostle announces, he will be happy to make good
what is owed.

"Charge it to me," he writes, "and I will pay for it."

The epistle ends with the Apostle assuring Philemon that
he has no doubt that his pleas will be honored, while promising
prayers that his friend in Colossae will ever be filled with "the
grace of the Lord Jesus Christ."

〜

The Roman sun was bright and hot as my priest-secretary and
I emerged from the Church of San Paolo alla Regola. The current pastor, another delightful priest of the Third Order of Saint
Francis, had shown us around and, just as his predecessor had
done for me and my fellow seminarians a half century before,
knocked on the door of Saint Paul's residence and feigned hearing a voice inviting him to enter.

"We have been doing this for a long, long time," he remarked
with a smile, "and I don't think we are ever likely to stop."

A Knock at the Door

Outside, after a thorough tour of San Paolo alla Regola, my priest-secretary and I walked across a cobblestone street and sat down on the porch of a coffee bar directly opposite the church. Together we read a short account of Paul and Onesimus in a little pamphlet we had purchased in the vestibule of the church. In it we learned that, according to Saint Ignatius of Antioch, Onesimus, after several years as a "freedman" in the home of Philemon, became the Bishop of Ephesus and ultimately a martyr for the Faith.

I put the pamphlet in my pocket and sent a "letter" to Saint Paul, and "Saint" Onesimus, too, in the form of a prayer. In it I begged them to ask the Divine Savior to inspire the clergy, religious, and laity of the Archdiocese of New York to participate in the Pauline Year by earnestly striving for a manner of life that includes not only the unbending commitment to the gospel for which the Apostle of the Gentiles is so well known, but also the unfailing compassion for those who are in fear and pain that the epistle to Philemon illustrates so mightily.

It was a request that I was quite confident the two saintly followers of the Lord would both understand and embrace.

New York, July 2008

Humble Beginnings

Our tale begins across the ocean. In 1783, the Holy See wanted to know if it could safely begin to organize the Catholic Church in the newly established United States of America. Accordingly, the papal nuncio to France approached Benjamin Franklin in Paris to ask him about the matter. Franklin assured the nuncio that there was no reason for hesitation or concern.

Nonetheless, the authorities in Rome felt it best to move slowly. Thus, they named a Jesuit priest from the Maryland prefect as the apostolic of the new nation, making him a kind of delegate of the Holy Father with limited episcopal powers, and directed him to study the situation of the clergy and laity in the thirteen original states so as to make a thorough report to Rome.

The priest's name was Father John Carroll. He came from one of the most distinguished families in the land. Indeed, a cousin of his signed the Declaration of Independence, and one of his brothers was among the framers of the Constitution. He was born in Maryland in 1736 but was educated for the priesthood in what is today Belgium, where, after ordination, he taught in the Jesuit colleges of Liège and Bruges. With the suppression of the Jesuits in 1773, he returned to Maryland to exercise his priesthood in the community where his family's home was located.

As prefect apostolic, Father Carroll proved to be extraordinarily energetic and effective. He carefully informed himself about the situation of Catholics in the United States; visited Maryland, Pennsylvania, and New York personally and repeatedly; and finally made a series of reports to Rome that proved to be of immense help to the decision makers in the Vatican.

When, in 1784, the shameful law in New York against the activity and even the presence of Catholic clergy was repealed, Father Carroll moved quickly. He put a priest in charge of all New York and eastern New Jersey and directed him to found a parish in New York City, which at the time was the second largest urban center in the nation after Philadelphia.

The parish was Saint Peter's, on Barclay Street in Lower Manhattan, which despite numerous difficulties and misunderstandings managed to survive and ultimately thrive. It is, of course, the parish that made us all so proud of its courageous priests and faithful in the wake of the tragedy of September 11, 2001.

⌒

Similar progress was made in the other major cities on the eastern seaboard. Thus, in 1789, Father Carroll was named the first bishop of the new Diocese of Baltimore, which was to serve all the United States, and was consecrated in Dorset, England, the following year.

His achievements in this new role were amazing. He called a national synod in 1791, in which were issued excellent norms regarding Church governance and the proper administration of the sacraments. He brought to the United States clergy from Europe and encouraged the founding of new communities of religious women. He created two Catholic colleges, Georgetown in Washington, D.C., and Mount Saint Mary's in Emmitsburg,

Maryland, and founded a major seminary as well. He wrote and spoke widely about the rights and duties of American citizens and, with uncommon charm and tact, sealed warm relationships with the political leaders of the day, including both George Washington and Thomas Jefferson.

Finally, after almost twenty years of presiding over the Church in the land he loved so dearly, the aging bishop succeeded in convincing the Holy See to divide his diocese so that the burgeoning Catholic population might be better served.

As a result, on April 8, 1808, Baltimore became an archdiocese, and four new suffragan dioceses were brought into being. For three of them Archbishop Carroll had candidates to present to Rome. They were Reverend Michael Egan for the Diocese of Philadelphia, Reverend Jean Cheverus for the Diocese of Boston, and Reverend Benedict Flaget for the Diocese of Bardstown in Kentucky, which in 1841 became the Diocese of Louisville.

To lead the new Diocese of New York, however, he had no one to propose. Hence, the choice was made by the Holy Father, Pope Pius VII, on the advice of his counselors in Rome. It fell to a Dominican priest who was the prior of the Church of Saint Clement in the heart of the Eternal City. His name was Reverend Richard Luke Concanen, and he was never to set foot in New York.

⁖

Richard Luke Concanen, the first bishop of New York, was born in Ireland in 1747. At the age of seventeen, he fled his native land to make his way to Italy, where, in 1770, he was ordained a Dominican priest in Rome's Lateran Basilica. For the next thirty-five years, Father Concanen held numerous positions of leadership in the Order of Preachers, all the while serving as "agent" in the Vatican for several bishops in England, Ireland, and the United States, one of them being Bishop Carroll of Baltimore.

The wars that followed upon the French Revolution and the ascendancy of Napoleon inflicted immense damage on the Church throughout Europe. Father Concanen steadfastly survived it all, along with the tragic pontificate of Pope Clement XIV, during which various religious orders, including the Jesuits, were suppressed, and even more harrowing pontificates of Pope Pius VI and Pope Pius VII, both of whom were imprisoned at various times by Napoleon to the horror of Catholics across the world. He watched England oppress Ireland and the Church in Ireland.

And to cap it all, he spent the last two years of his life, from 1808 to 1810, trying to gain passage to New York in the face of embargoes by both the English and the French, which rendered travel to the United States virtually impossible.

On June 19, 1810, Bishop Concanen, who had been consecrated in Rome in April of 1808, died in Naples after having been prevented a few days earlier by French naval officers from boarding a ship that the bishop knew to be destined for New York. He was buried the next day in a Neapolitan church dedicated to Saint Joseph where few, if any, even knew who he was.

≈⌒

Bishop Concanen's saga, however, does not end here. One hundred sixty-eight years later, on July 9, 1978, to be exact, a plaque identifying him as the first bishop of New York was attached to his tomb and blessed by one of his successors, Terence Cardinal Cooke. The plaque had been brought from New York to Naples by the cardinal, who was accompanied by two of his auxiliary bishops, Anthony F. Mestice and Patrick V. Ahern.

The plaque was set in place and blessed at the conclusion of a Mass for the repose of the soul of Bishop Concanen, celebrated by the cardinal and the two auxiliary bishops. As they were leaving the church, they unexpectedly met a Catholic chaplain of the United States Navy whose ship was anchored in the harbor of Naples. In the course of their conversation with the chaplain, they suggested that he might want to visit the tomb of the first bishop of New York and see the plaque that adorned it.

This the chaplain did, and thus another of Bishop Concanen's successors knelt in prayer before his final resting place. The chaplain's name was Reverend John J. O'Connor.[13]

New York, April 2006

---

[13] John Cardinal O'Connor succeeded Terence Cardinal Cooke as archbishop of New York in 1984. Cardinal Egan, in turn, succeeded Cardinal O'Connor in 2000.

Her "Magic"

Not even a whisper of a breeze flowed through the old Gothic church in the heart of the South Bronx. It was a Saturday afternoon in July. I had just finished my homily and was making my way back to the ornate wooden chair behind the altar.

In the first pew on my left were six young men whom I was to ordain deacons for service in the Missionaries of Charity of Mother Teresa of Calcutta. In the first pew on the right were seven Sisters of Mother Teresa's congregation, and Mother Teresa herself.

As I rose to begin the Offertory of the Mass, a shriek was heard from the rear of the church. A man of perhaps thirty-five years of age, shirtless and bleeding profusely from his face and neck, charged up the aisle. In his left hand he frantically waved a torn T-shirt scarlet with blood.

Arriving at the head of the aisle and shouting all the while, he stumbled, fell, and hit his forehead on the first marble stair leading into the sanctuary. I stood aghast. What does one do in such a situation?

Before an answer came, Mother Teresa slipped from her pew, took hold of the man's bloody hands, and cradled him in her arms. Quietly and calmly, four Missionaries of Charity joined her in the aisle and with incredible ease lifted the man and carried him into the sacristy on my right. Throughout it all I could hear him, first shouting and then sobbing, "Help me. Help me, somebody. I need help."

The sacristy door swung closed. I continued the Offertory, stretching out the prayers and the incensing as long as I could. Just before the "Holy, Holy, Holy," Mother and her Sisters emerged from the sacristy and glided into their pew. The ordination ceremony continued as though nothing unusual had taken place.

After the final blessing, the clergy led me down the aisle. In the vestibule, I congratulated the newly ordained and their families and friends and then returned to the sanctuary to collect my liturgical books and the other accouterments I had brought with me for the ceremony.

All of these I carried into the sacristy, where Mother Teresa and her Sisters were speaking with an excited group of men and women from the neighborhood. I approached Mother, smiled, and, not knowing what to do, bowed a kind of Indian bow in her direction. She turned toward me, but I could not be sure whether she responded to my gesture. For she was so short and I so tall that I could not see her face. I bowed again rather awkwardly and moved away from the group.

$\approx$

The pastor of the parish, a priest whom I knew from several meetings shortly after my arrival the year before as an auxiliary bishop of the Archdiocese of New York, approached and drew me aside.

"The man who disturbed the ceremony is no stranger here," he reported. "He did the same thing last Sunday and the Sunday before that. We had to call the police on both occasions. No one could calm him down. He is being pursued by drug dealers. They like to keep addicts like him under control with occasional knifings."

I did not know what to respond, so the pastor went on.

"You should have seen Mother Teresa with him here in the sacristy this afternoon. It was like magic. She cleaned the blood off his face and neck, stroked his head over and over, folded his hands in hers; and I think she had him praying. It was like magic. Maybe I shouldn't say 'magic,' but you know what I mean. A kind of wondrous, loving miracle. We didn't call the police this time. We didn't need to."

Again, I was without words. Hence, gathering up my belongings, I shook the pastor's hand and began to move toward the exit leading from the sacristy to the outside of the church. As one of the altar servers opened the door, I could see the intense July heat rising in trembling waves from the glistening white sidewalk.

"Where are you going, Bishop?" a voice behind me inquired. It belonged to a stocky man in his twenties whom I had noticed in the sacristy when I entered.

"Over to catch the subway," I replied. "I live in Midtown Manhattan."

"I have a van parked around the corner," he announced. "Let me give you a lift home."

There was no need to press the offer. "Great!" I exclaimed. "I would welcome a ride if I am not taking you too far out of your way. This heat is tremendous."

"No problem," he declared, taking from my hands the suitcase that contained my vestments and the wooden box in which my crozier was stowed.

"This way," he added, and I followed most gratefully.

As we made our way south to the residence for retired priests in which I lived on 34th Street and First Avenue, the young man spoke almost without taking a breath. He was captivated by the ordination ceremony. He had prayed intensely for the six new deacons. And he could not stop marveling at the way Mother Teresa and her Sisters had handled the drug addict.

"The priest who was speaking with you in the sacristy had it right," he repeated over and over. "There is something magical about that woman. If she hadn't been there, the police would have been called, and then the man would have been back in jail probably for the umpteenth time. But she knew what to do. She gave him love. She treated him like a prince.

"Maybe 'magic' isn't the right word, but it's not far off the mark," he concluded. "Grace magic. Heavenly magic. Something like that."

We parked in front of my residence. He shut off the motor but kept the air conditioner running. He needed to talk. He needed to tell someone how deeply moved he was by what he had witnessed. And I listened with pleasure, for to me his soliloquy seemed almost a prayer.

"I'm keeping you too long, Bishop," he said.

"Not at all," I answered. "If I hadn't met you, I would still be on the subway. Thanks a million for everything. You have been most kind."

We shook hands. I opened the car door and stepped out into the street, never expecting to see the young man again.

Six years later, I ordained him a priest for the Diocese of Bridgeport.

Bridgeport, October 1997

The First Christmas Card

Holy Cross Parish on the periphery of Rome is immense. Indeed, it is so immense that, scattered within its boundaries are several chapels smaller than the main parish church, but serving rather large congregations all the same.

One of them is dedicated to Santa Angelina, seats around four hundred, and is attached to a daycare center conducted by a community of dedicated religious women. Until I left Rome in 1985, it was my privilege and joy to celebrate the Masses and hear confessions on weekends in this little-known corner of the Lord's Roman vineyard.

Early in December of 1984, I was standing one Sunday morning in front of the chapel chatting with members of the congregation as they were departing after the eleven o'clock Mass. Out of the corner of my eye, I noticed a man of about thirty years of age who had stationed himself just inside the door of the chapel. I suspected that he was waiting to speak with me, and my suspicion proved to be correct.

"Father," he whispered as I approached him, "I need to speak with you. It's urgent."

We went into a parlor in the Sisters' convent and sat down, each in an overstuffed chair. The introductions were brief. He was anxious to get right to the point.

Ten years earlier, he and his wife were married. They had been engaged but had to advance the date of their wedding because she was pregnant. Shortly thereafter, he was offered an excellent position overseas. They left their families, moved to a land where neither he nor she spoke the language, rented an apartment, and within a few months were forced to return home because the company that had hired him was in financial trouble.

Back in Italy, she had her child "discreetly" in the home of relatives south of Rome and, finally, after an extended stay with other relatives in the same area, returned to the Eternal City, where he had found a job. The job, however, paid poorly, and the family was therefore forced to live in what the man in the other overstuffed chair described as "a very humble home."

"We're ashamed to have our parents visit us," he told me, his face turning red with hurt and resentment, "so last night my wife and I agreed to put an end to our marriage. She's going back to live with her parents and filing for divorce, and I don't care. I can hardly believe it, Father, but I frankly don't care."

A knock came at the parlor door. It was one of the Sisters, asking if we would like some coffee. I replied that we would and nervously cleared my throat.

"Forgive me," I said in a tone that was as hushed and unchallenging as I could manage, "but I believe you do care. Your trembling voice and your angry eyes give you away. Permit me, please, to tell you why you care.

"The cinema, the nighttime soap operas from America, the magazines on the newsstands, and a large sector of the daily papers," I observed, "are striving to convince us all that marriage is a passing and trivial matter. Happily, however, they are facing an uphill battle with people who have even the most rudimentary understanding of what married life is all about.

"Marriage," I continued, "is a truly wondrous reality. On their wedding day, a man and a woman give to and receive from each other the permanent and exclusive right to do something of unique grandeur and beauty, which is, of course, to perform together an act of love from which can result a person, an image and likeness of God, a being for whom the very Son of God would die.

"Nor can we human beings make little of marriage, its meaning, and its dignity for long without severely damaging ourselves in the process. Make it acceptable to break the bond of marriage with casual divorce, and await incalculable harm for all involved. The wife will find herself without security. The husband will find himself without stability. The children will find themselves without guidance. And society will find itself crumbling.

"No thinking person may rightly 'not care' about the tragic ending of a marriage," I concluded. "There is simply too much at stake."

꩜

The coffee arrived. We thanked the Sister, and slowly sipped it in silence. Suddenly, my friend spoke up.

"I am not going to argue with any of that," he said with a tinge of bitterness in his voice. "But what about marriages like mine, marriages that start badly and never seem to find their way? All the theory, theology, or whatever get lost when you go up the aisle before you plan to because your fiancée is pregnant; when you live the first months of your married life in a foreign land; when your son has to be born away from home; and when, after ten years, you cannot give your family anything better than a very humble home, a home so humble that you don't want your parents or your wife's parents to come for a visit."

He put his head in his hands. His shoulders were shaking, and he was digging his heels into the legs of the overstuffed chair.

It was no time for preaching. The situation, rather, seemed to call for a story. I told, therefore, of a teenage girl engaged to a young man, of her being found with child, and of their being married under the most embarrassing of circumstances. I told of the birth of their son in a shelter for animals and of years of exile in Egypt, a land whose language and culture were unknown to both spouses. And, I finished by observing that the head of the household, Joseph by name, was not, as some have thought, a carpenter but rather a "joiner of wood," which is to say a construction laborer who very likely gave Mary, his wife, and her Son a home far humbler than any to be found in Rome's Holy Cross Parish.

My friend rose awkwardly, shook my hand unenthusiastically, murmured a few words that I did not understand, and left me alone in the parlor.

The next Sunday, and for many Sundays thereafter, I observed the man with whom I had spoken in the convent parlor attending Mass in the Chapel of Santa Angelina, accompanied by a woman and a boy of ten years or so. He never failed to wave at me when leaving the chapel. Still, it was clear that he wanted no further contact. If I happened to catch his eye before Mass or during the homily, he would nod politely and turn away immediately. All of this perplexed me at first, but in time became lost in other concerns.

⌒

The following May, I was named an auxiliary bishop of the Archdiocese of New York, and cards and letters of good wishes were arriving in surprising numbers. To help me handle the correspondence and the arrangements for the ceremony of episcopal consecration, an English lady who lived in Rome came each morning to my office, opened the mail, set aside what needed a reply, and generally kept things in order. Blessed with a delightful sense of humor, she had a quip for every occasion.

"Well, fancy this," she cried one day as I was working at my desk. "You just received the first Christmas card of 1985. Merry Christmas, and in case I may have forgotten, Happy Saint Patrick's Day, too."

With that, she handed me a sheet of typing paper that had been folded into the form of a greeting card. On the front of it there was pasted a picture of the Nativity with the stable smudged in black ink to make it look even more unappealing than the artist had intended.

The message inside the card read as follows: "Best wishes, dear Bishop. Before you leave for America, there is something you should know. Like that other couple in a very humble home, my wife and I will be staying together. Thank you for reminding me about them, and thank you especially for caring."

The loyal subject of the British Crown left my office just as I started reading the card. I breathed a prayer of thanks. For she would have had way too much fun joshing me about the tears I was fighting back.

New York, December 2003

Just Three Pages

The corridor was dark. I could hardly find the door of the room to which I had been assigned. It was late in October, and the Roman rains had begun to fall. I removed my wet coat and sat down on a well-worn cot.

This is where I had come the year before for my annual retreat, and I was happy to return. The building, located on the Via Merulana in the center of the Eternal City, housed the offices of the general of the Redemptorist Fathers, a church in which the original painting of Our Lady of Perpetual Help is to be found, and two corridors of little rooms, perhaps "cells" would be the more accurate term, for priest retreatants like myself.

Down the corridor from my room was the apartment in which Alphonsus Liguori, the patron saint of Moral Theologians, had lived and worked in the mid-1700s. During this period of my own life, the early 1960s, I was a tutor who gave classes ("Repetitor" was the official title) for students in the American seminary on the edge of Vatican City; and my field was moral theology. Hence, the proximity of the apartment of Saint Alphonsus meant a great deal to me. Often during the meditation periods I would wander down to his end of the corridor to sense and enjoy a rather special closeness.

This particular year, however, it was another Redemptorist, not yet a canonized saint, who made the retreat altogether memorable.

Shortly after arriving in my room, and while I was still seated on the cot, wondering how long it would take for my shoes and clothes to dry, a knock came at the door. Before I could respond with the customary Italian "*Avanti*," a priest quite advanced in years entered, carrying an electric tape recorder with a book balanced on top. He placed the recorder on an antiquated wooden table and plugged its long extension cord into an outlet attached to the lone light that hung from the center of the ceiling.

"There is no one to give the retreatants conferences this week," he announced in English with a distinct German accent. "So, I will be your director, and what you must do is this. Listen to a section of these tapes each morning and each afternoon, and in the evening come to my room at 6:30 for a discussion to end the day."

He leaned over to the table and took from it the book that lay atop the tape recorder. "Also, you must read this book from cover to cover," he declared. "Toward the end, I have marked three pages for special attention. We will discuss them, just these three pages, when the retreat is over."

With that he rose, shook my hand, and took his leave. I do not recall that he told me his name. Still, I had no trouble discovering it, for it was written in white paint on the side of the recorder along with directions to his room.

⌣

For the next four days, I did as I had been instructed: tapes in the morning and afternoon, followed by a conference with my director before supper each evening. The tapes were in Italian and not much to my taste. The book, on the other hand, was thoroughly fascinating.

It was a rather lengthy biography of a bishop by the name of John Neumann. He was born in Bohemia in 1811 and entered the seminary in 1831. When he completed his studies five years later, his bishop refused to ordain him because of a surplus of priests. Thus, with one suit of clothes, a letter of recommendation from his pastor, and a few dollars in his pocket, Neumann sailed for the United States in 1836, hoping to find a bishop who would accept him for ordination.

Within a few days after his arrival, the hope was fulfilled when Bishop John Dubois of New York, in urgent need of a priest to serve an ever-growing number of German-speaking immigrants, agreed to ordain the multilingual immigrant from Bohemia.

Six years later, having obtained the permission of his bishop, Neumann became the first professed Redemptorist priest in the United States and soon thereafter was named pastor of the Parish of Saint Alphonsus Liguori in Baltimore. From there, in 1852, he was transferred to Philadelphia as its fourth bishop.

Throughout his tenure in the City of Brotherly Love, Neumann, who was small of stature and spoke with a considerable accent, was never accepted by the social leadership of the community. Nonetheless, in scarcely eight years he established eighty new parishes, organized the most extraordinary parochial school system in the nation, created an extensive chain of charitable institutions, founded a seminary, built a cathedral, championed Eucharistic devotion, wrote catechisms in several languages, and even published commentaries on the Old and New Testaments.

"But none of this is what made Bishop Neumann the splendid disciple of Jesus Christ that he was," my director intoned as we discussed the biography during our last meeting together. "One day he will be recognized by the Church as a saint of God, and the reason is in just the three pages that I marked. Did you read those pages carefully? Did you understand their message?"

Since the rain had not let up for four days and I could not go out into the tiny garden that I had enjoyed the year before, I had read the pages over and again, mostly in my room. The tale that they told was powerful.

⌒⌒

In the northern reaches of the Diocese of Philadelphia, in a small town by the name of Bellefonte, there lived an elderly Benedictine priest serving an impoverished parish. Twelve days before the Christmas of 1859, Bishop Neumann received a package from the priest along with a note reporting that the parish rectory had burned to the ground. None of the priest's few possessions had survived apart from his chalice, which he implored the bishop to have repaired and returned to him, if possible, in time for Christmas.

Neumann saw to the repair, and directed one of his priests to take the chalice to the post office to be sent to Bellefonte. Three days after Christmas, a frantic message came from the Benedictine pastor. What had become of his most precious, indeed, his only remaining possession?

Although suffering from shortness of breath and chronic dizzy spells, on a cold winter's evening Bishop Neumann made his way to the post office, discovered the chalice in a storeroom, and had it sent on to its owner. As he went out into the street, he felt ill, struggled to catch his breath in the icy wind, and some minutes later was found dead in the snow.

Carried into the private residence of a Protestant woman who thought he might be a vagrant, he was laid out on a couch;

and his hands were pulled from within the pockets of his coat. Clutched in one was the receipt for the chalice, and in the other a Rosary.

"What made him the splendid disciple of the Lord that he was?" my director demanded. "I will tell you. Not the parishes, not the schools, not the catechisms, not the cathedral or the seminary. No, it was rather a quality of soul that must distinguish every priest, indeed, every follower of Jesus Christ. And that quality is kindness — the willingness to feel the pain of others, to care for others, even to sacrifice oneself for others. Neumann died doing a kindness that no one would have expected of a person in his position. And, he died doing that kindness because he had lived a life of kindness."

He pointed his finger at me in a gesture which Americans often find disagreeable, but which Europeans regularly employ to drive home a point. "Be kind, Father," he said, "and you will be living the Gospel. That is the secret of John Neumann. That is the secret of those three pages."

He rose, told me to keep the biography, and signaled that our meeting had come to an end. I gathered up my belongings, and went out into the unrelenting rain.

⁀

Three years ago, I was again in Rome in late October. On another stormy evening, I made my way to the church on the Via Merulana where the original of the painting of Our Lady of Perpetual Help is to be found. I had agreed to meet a friend there so that we might go out together for supper.

My friend was late, and the sacristan was beginning to lock the church doors. I told him that I would continue to wait in the coffee bar across the street.

"No, Father," he protested, "you better stay in here. There's a real tempest outside."

My friend finally arrived, and I went into the sacristy to thank the sacristan for his consideration. He beckoned me over to a cabinet with a large, polished counter attached. On the counter lay two metal capsules, each about the size of a half-dollar coin. They were fitted with glass covers; and when I looked closely, I could see that one was a relic of Saint Alphonsus Liguori and the other of *Saint* John Neumann.[14]

"You're a bishop, aren't you?" the sacristan whispered with a knowing smile. "I can tell from your ring. Please take one of these relics as a remembrance of your visit to our church."

In the face of such kindness, I had no trouble making my choice. It was determined by just three pages that I had read over and over during another rainy October in the same holy place.

Bridgeport, July 1997

---

[14] Saint John Neumann (1811–1860) was canonized by Pope Paul VI on June 19, 1977.

The Thief's Sacrifice

He was almost eighty-five, and for over ten years had been retired from active priestly service. Still, each Saturday, weather permitting, he took two buses from the retirement home in which he lived to the church he had built as a pastor many years before, so that he might attend the afternoon Mass.

"I wish I could concelebrate with the priest," he told me, "but I can't. The eyes and the knees aren't what they used to be. But, there's no problem. I offer Mass the way the Good Thief did."

"What do you mean by that?" I inquired.

"Haven't you ever read the collected sermons of Saint John Vianney, the Curé of Ars?" he demanded with feigned surprise.

"To be honest, no," I answered rather lamely.

"Well, I must get you a copy," he said. "In one of his most famous sermons, the saint preaches about the Old Testament prophet Malachi and explains how the Holy Sacrifice of the Mass is to be offered by those who are not the celebrants. If you read it, you will understand." A playful smile lit up his face. "I must get you a copy," he repeated. "All of the priests of my era had one."

The years passed, my friend was called to Heaven, and our conversation about the Mass and the Good Thief slipped back into the dark corridors of my memory. A few months ago, however, I received in the mail an advertisement for a reprint of *The Collected Sermons of the Curé of Ars.*

"This classic was first published in the United States in 1901," the advertisement read. "It has been an inspiration to generations of priests and deserves a place in the libraries of all Catholic clergy today."

I ordered it and, upon receipt, immediately set myself to looking for a sermon having to do with the prophet Malachi.

It turned out to be the one that Saint John Vianney had composed for the Second Sunday of Pentecost, according to the old liturgical calendar. He entitled it "Holy Mass" and indicated as its Scriptural source the words of Malachi in the first chapter of his prophetic book: "In every place there is a sacrifice, and there is offered to my name a clean oblation."

The sermon opens by stating that, as sinful creatures, we are by nature led to offer sacrifices to the Creator in reparation for our offenses against His holy will. This was done in Old Testament times by Moses, Abraham, Melchizedek, and others. However, the sermon went on, "another sacrifice, holier and purer, which would continue to the end of the world," was needed—the sacrifice offered on the Cross by "Jesus Christ, Who is God, like the Father, and man, as one of us."

The new sacrifice, the Curé continued, is repeated day after day during Holy Mass, wherein the Son of God is both Priest and Victim, just as He was on Calvary. The only difference is in the manner of the sacrificing. At Mass, it is unbloody. The Body of the Redeemer, which was scourged, nailed, and pierced, and the Blood of the Redeemer, which poured forth from His hands, feet, and side, are hidden under the appearance of bread and wine.

They are, therefore, in the words of the Curé, seen only "with eyes of faith, not with the eyes of our head." Moreover, a merely human priest stands in the place of the Lord as an instrument of His in the sacrificing, so that a "clean oblation" might continue to be offered across the ages "from the rising of the sun even to the going down thereof," as the prophet Malachi expressed it.

"Holy Mass," Saint John Vianney announces, "is the sacrifice of the most adorable Body and Blood of Jesus Christ.... [It] was instituted on Maundy Thursday when the Lord took bread and transformed it into His Body, and then taking wine, changed it into His Blood." The Savior, however, did not stop there, the Curé insists. Rather, on the same Maundy Thursday, He gave His Apostles and their successors the wondrous "authority" to do exactly what He Himself was to do on the Cross.

⌒

Suddenly, the course of the sermon changes. We know how the Savior offered His sacrifice, our preacher observes; and we know how the priest offers his. But, we may not be clear about how we are to offer our sacrifice when we join the Lord and His priest at the altar. We may not understand that each of us is to present to the Father in Heaven, through His Son, a sacrifice of "all that we are — our body, our soul, our possessions, and even our life."

Certainly, none of this should come as a surprise to us today. *The Constitution on the Sacred Liturgy* of the Second Vatican Council, for instance, states it all quite clearly in the chapter on the Mass, where we read:

> The Church earnestly desires that Christ's faithful, when present at this mystery of faith, not be there as strangers or silent spectators. On the contrary, through a proper

appreciation of the rites and prayers, they should participate knowingly, devoutly, and actively. They should be instructed by God's word and refreshed at the table of the Lord's Body. They should give thanks to God ... and by offering the Immaculate Victim, not only through the hands of the priests, but also with him, they should learn to *offer themselves too*. (48)

Nor is this conciliar doctrine something new. In Pope Pius XII's encyclical letter *Mediator Dei*, issued in 1947, and frequently cited by the Council, for example, we are taught:

It is desirable that all the faithful be aware that to participate in the Eucharistic Sacrifice is their chief duty and supreme dignity.... Together with Christ and through Him let them make their oblation, and in union with Him let them *offer up themselves*. (80)

Nonetheless, the image with which the Curé of Ars drives all of this home is marvelously original and compelling. The Good Thief, he proclaims, shows us how we are to "behave" at Mass "from the Offertory to the Consecration, when we offer ourselves up to God with Jesus Christ."

Bound to a cross and unable to move, he had only his heart and his tongue to present to the Lord in sacrifice; and he offered both totally when he championed the Savior against the blasphemy of the other thief and prayed to be remembered by the dying Christ when He came into His "kingdom."

In the presence of the Lord's sacrifice on Calvary, a sinner, indeed, a hardened criminal, was moved to offer to his God all that he had and was. The same needs to happen, the Curé declares, at every Mass in which we participate, whether as celebrants or not. We are to hand over all that we are in sacrifice to the Lord; and we are to trust that the result will be an outpouring, perhaps a miracle, of grace.

⁓

The church that my priest friend used to visit on Saturday afternoon "to offer Mass the way the Good Thief did" is an imposing edifice on a busy street. A few weeks ago I was in the neighborhood and stopped by to say a prayer.

I knelt in the pew closest to the Twelfth Station and fixed my gaze on the thief to the right of the Lord.

"When my eyes and knees aren't what they used to be and I take my place among the faithful at Holy Mass," I told him, "may I have long since learned to give myself completely to my God, as you did. May I know, as you knew, how to offer all that I am and have to Christ, and with Christ, in sacrifice."

Bridgeport, May 1997

The Goad

At home, his name was Saul. On the street, it was Paul. His father was a Jew of the tribe of Benjamin, an exponent of the Pharisee party, and a tentmaker by trade.

At the age of six, Saul was enrolled in a Jewish elementary school where he learned to read and love the Hebrew Scriptures or, as we would say today, the books of the Old Testament.

There is some division among authors about Saul's "high school" education. Some suggest he had none of a formal kind. Others maintain he was blessed with excellent secondary-school training in an institution that introduced him to the best of Greco-Roman culture. Given the ease with which he quoted such classic poets and philosophers as Aratus, Epimenides, and Menander in sermons and writings, most are inclined to favor the second opinion.

Whatever of this, at the age of sixteen or seventeen, Saul was sent to Jerusalem for what was the "Ivy League" education of a Jew in the Middle East at the time. It was directed by the Pharisee Gamaliel, and like "Ivy League" alumni of all eras, Paul, who was undoubtedly known as Saul in his student days, did not hesitate to remind his followers what a splendid intellectual formation he had had. ("I [was] ... brought up in this city at the feet of Gamaliel, educated according to the strict manner of the law of our fathers." [Acts 22:3].)

Having completed his studies under the tutelage of Gamaliel at around the age of twenty, Saul returned to his hometown of Tarsus in the Roman Province of Cilicia. Tarsus was then considered one of the most important commercial and cultural centers of the world, ranking behind only Athens and Alexandria. Today, it is an impoverished village a few miles north of the south-central coast of Turkey.

There, in his father's establishment, Saul plied the tentmaking trade along with what appears to have been a good number of employees, turning hemp into canvas and canvas into tents and sails. Here, too, he enjoyed the dignity and privileges of Roman citizenship, thanks, it would seem, to an enterprising grandfather, who had either won it for special services to the government or purchased it, as many well-to-do businessmen did in that era of the Roman Empire.

At the age of thirty, Saul returned to Jerusalem to work with the Jewish leadership to put an end to a movement that preached what was then called "the Way" and what we would today identify as the gospel. Like many other devout Jews, he was outraged by the claim of the movement that the eagerly awaited Messiah had actually come and ended his life as a criminal on a cross. For Saul, this was a blasphemy of the most egregious kind.

Accordingly, with the endorsement of local authorities, Saul searched out all involved in the movement with the intention of having them arrested and, if they refused to mend their ways, imprisoned and even executed. Years later, he confessed that he had willingly engaged in all of this and was even an enthusiastic observer as Saint Stephen, the first Christian martyr, was stoned to death for preaching the gospel of the crucified Messiah. ("And when the blood of Stephen ... was shed, I also was standing by and approving, and keeping the garments of those who killed him" [Acts 22:20].)

While in Jerusalem, however, Saul learned that the Way had spread to the capital city of Syria, Damascus, and was attracting a large number of converts from Judaism. Thus, with new letters of authorization from religious authorities, he traveled to Damascus, along with several companions. The journey lasted at least eight days, one of them being a Sabbath, on which the pious Jew from Tarsus undoubtedly rested.

⁓

A short distance from the city gates, Saul was enveloped in a brilliant light and, falling to the ground, heard a voice saying, "Saul, Saul, why do you persecute me? It hurts you to kick against the goad." To the voice, he replied, "Who are you, Lord?" And the answer came back loud and clear: "I am Jesus whom you are persecuting" (cf. Acts 26:14–15).

All of this is quite clear and familiar, except for the remark about the goad, which, perhaps, requires a bit of commentary.

In the Middle East at the time of Saint Paul, fields were prepared for seeding by means of heavy wooden plows pulled by oxen that were kept moving forward with the help of a goad, a sharp-pointed stick against which the animals would regularly kick, even though it dug painfully into their legs.

Is it possible that Saul was already having second thoughts about what he was doing to the followers of the Way? Might he have begun not only to admire their courage and commitment, but also to wonder about the validity of their beliefs?

Most commentators whose works I have studied would suggest that such was very likely the case, and I do not hesitate to agree.

In any event, we move on to note that Saul was heard to cry out, "What shall I do, Lord?" (Acts 22:10). And, again, the answer came back loud and clear: "Rise and enter the city, and you will be told what you are to do" (Acts 9:6).

Accordingly, having lost his sight in the blast of light that had engulfed him, a deeply shaken Saul was led by the hand into Damascus by those who had accompanied him on his journey.

Gravely concerned about their friend's condition, his companions brought him to the home of a certain Judas, who lived on the main thoroughfare of the city, a street called Straight. Three days later, Saul, who during this period "neither ate nor drank" (Acts 9:9), was visited by a follower of the Way who laid his hands on him, cured him of his blindness, and baptized him.

The tale ends rather undramatically: "Then he ... took food and was strengthened" (Acts 9:19).

⇜

Somewhat less than two thousand years later, I was in Damascus with a group of classmates from my seminary in Rome. We were coming to the end of a month-long tour of "the lands of the Bible" and were seated on ancient stone benches that lined the street called Straight, listening to a priest read the account of the conversion of Saint Paul in chapter 22 of the Acts of the Apostles.

When the priest, who was also a distinguished New Testament scholar, came to the statement about kicking against the goads, one of our number asked what it meant. The priest offered essentially the interpretation that was suggested above. Yet, he immediately added as a kind of sidebar, one of the most celebrated anti-Christian historians of the late nineteenth century,

Ernest Renan, had spent several years of his life "kicking the goad" about the entire story.

"He 'earnestly' wanted to discredit it," the priest declared with a twinkle in his eye, "but found this very hard to do. For the story, which is recounted by Saint Luke in chapter 9 of Acts, is reported in chapter 22 as told by Paul to an angry crowd gathered before the Temple of Jerusalem and in chapter 26 as told again by Paul to King Agrippa and a Roman procurator by the name of Porcius Festus.

"And all of this was written down and widely disseminated throughout the Middle East within thirty years," the priest continued. "If it were an invention, it would have been quickly and easily 'debunked' by countless individuals and groups who would have felt that disproving it would be very much in their interest.

"So what did our celebrated historian Ernest Renan do?" the priest asked. "Faced by inconvenient facts, he abandoned the basic rules of the science of history and came up with what follows in a book titled *Les Apôtres*. Paul was extremely tired as he approached Damascus. The sun was beating down on him, and he was being tormented within by self-hatred because of his involvement in the martyrdom of Saint Stephen. The tiredness, the sun, and the torment suddenly came together to overpower him, and he began to hallucinate. There was no light surrounding him. There was no voice to which he responded. The event was nothing more than an episode of what we today would call a 'psychotic seizure.'

"This," the priest announced, fixing his eyes on each of us, "is 'kicking against the goad' in style. But don't laugh. It is something we are all at least tempted to do at various times in our lives. We understand exactly what the Lord has revealed and exactly what He expects of us as a result. Nonetheless, we concoct all sorts of half-baked suppositions that maybe we have mistaken His meaning or His demands in the hope of somehow eluding them. In short, we 'kick against the goad,' as Paul was very likely doing before his conversion, as Renan clearly did in his account of that conversion, and — lest we forget — as dumb oxen always do when pulling the plow.

"In his Second Epistle to Timothy, Saint Paul proclaims that 'all Scripture is inspired by God and useful for teaching,'" the priest concluded. "And this is one of the lessons those four little words, 'kicking against the goad,' were meant to teach. Keep in mind, and throughout your lives have the courage to face head-on the reality of what God has told us and the reality of what He requires of us. This is not only psychologically healthy; it is also a key to holiness."

Years ago, as a seminarian, I purchased an unbound copy of Renan's *Les Apôtres* in a secondhand bookstore on the bank of the Seine River in Paris, but unfortunately I lost it in the course of numerous transfers as a priest from assignment to assignment. Last week, I borrowed a copy from our seminary library, and, one night, I sat down and read the chapter about the conversion of Saint Paul, not once, but three times.

As I closed the book, I asked the Apostle to the Gentiles to speak with the Lord about keeping me from "goad-kicking." Somehow, I felt he would be happy to do so.

New York, September 2008

Pope John Paul II: A Personal Portrait

Two weeks ago, the editor of the *Fairfield County Catholic* sent me a note asking that I write an article for a special edition of the newspaper celebrating the twentieth anniversary of the election of Pope John Paul II. "It would be great if you could share with our readers a personal portrait of the Pontiff based on your various encounters with him," he wrote. "We all know how much you admire our beloved Holy Father."

What follows is my response.

⌒

My first "encounter" with Pope John Paul II was at a distance, and it occurred several years before his election as the 264th Successor of Saint Peter. In the mid-1970s, the Office of the Secretary of State in the Vatican asked me, at that time a judge of the Tribunal of the Sacred Roman Rota, to join a group of clergy and laity who were to visit Moscow and Zagorsk, a city outside of Moscow that is popularly known as the "Vatican of the Russian Orthodox Church." A guide and an interpreter from the Council for Promoting Christian Unity were provided, and I was directed to bring with me the distinctive vesture of a Rota judge, which I was to wear at a dinner to be arranged for me with the Patriarch of the Russian Orthodox Church, who was also a member of the Supreme Soviet.

Although I was a bit unnerved by the assignment, everything worked out very well, indeed.

Upon returning to Rome, I gave the cardinal secretary of state a detailed rundown of all that I had seen and heard, along with a bulky box of gifts from the Patriarch and the various hierarchs who had been at the dinner table with us. At the conclusion of our conversation, the cardinal thanked me profusely for my report and expressed hope that I had enjoyed my brief Russian adventure.

What we saw and heard in the Soviet Union was, of course, both informative and fascinating. Yet it paled in comparison with what we experienced one morning in Poland where, allegedly for diplomatic reasons, we stopped on our way to Moscow. Having visited Warsaw, Czestochowa, and Kraków, on the last day of our Polish sojourn we were invited to tour an industrial town near Kraków that, incredibly, appeared to be a source of pride for our official Communist guides, who repeatedly defined themselves as our "hosts."

The town was called Nowa Huta (New Town), and it might have been the setting for the bleakest of Orwellian novels. It had been built to house laborers in the Togliatti steelworks and consisted of block after block of ugly gray apartment complexes, many of which looked as though they were about to crumble. On the day of our visit, the rain fell incessantly, and rivulets of muddy water flowed freely over the poorly paved streets.

Our guide from the Vatican insisted that we go immediately to the only church in the town, where a Franciscan friar was waiting to recount the history of the edifice, much to the annoyance of our "hosts."

The church, the friar told us, was built by the people of the area out of stones carried one by one from the bed of a nearby river. From the outset, however, the government was adamant that Nowa Huta would never be allowed to have a house of worship and regularly bulldozed early efforts at construction. Finally, the friar reported, after numerous confrontations between local authorities and the people, a contingent of police shot and killed several of the builders when they refused to halt their work.

At this juncture, the friar went on, "The archbishop of Kraków took matters in hand. He came here. He organized the people. He stared down the villains, and the villains were forced to relent. Thus, Nowa Huta is blessed with a splendid church," the friar concluded triumphantly, "because the faithful of Nowa Huta are blessed with a great archbishop, who is a man of limitless courage."

On a page concerning Nowa Huta in my guidebook, I entered the name of the courageous archbishop as "Votilla," and expected that I would never hear that name again.

⌒)

My second "encounter" with Pope John Paul II was, like the first, at a distance. It took place while I was working in the aforementioned Tribunal of the Sacred Roman Rota. The dean of the Rota was Polish and well up in years. One afternoon he telephoned to ask if I could drive him to a spiritual retreat that was to be conducted the following week for Pope Paul VI and officials of the Roman Curia. Since I was not among those invited to attend, I struggled to come up with a reason to decline the dean's request.

"My car is quite small," I declared rather lamely.

Practice for Heaven

"That makes no difference at all," the dean retorted. "I want you to hear the retreat master. Please pick me up at eight-thirty next Monday morning."

The car in question was a secondhand Fiat 127, whose four tiny cylinders always seemed to be performing at their limit. Nonetheless, I appeared at the dean's residence at the appointed hour and helped him into the front seat. "*C'est une belle voiture* [It's a fine car]," he proclaimed in French, one of the three languages he regularly used all at once, depending on whether his thought could best be expressed in the tongue of Cicero, Dante, or Molière.

The retreat was held in an uncommonly dark chapel inside the Papal Palace. Pope Paul VI knelt in the sacristy on the right and briefly greeted the retreatants after all had taken their places in the pews. In due course, a tall, strapping cardinal came out of the sacristy on the left, approached the altar, knelt for an unusually long time before the tabernacle, and finally made his way to the podium. He spoke in clear, although accented, Italian, and what he had to say was nothing short of electrifying.

As we filed out of the chapel, the comments were exclamations of admiration and amazement. Everyone wanted to know the cardinal's background and how to pronounce his name.

~

As we drove back to his residence, the dean could scarcely contain his pride in our retreat master and his countryman, Karol Cardinal Wojtyla. Over and again, he repeated the spiritual insights we had gleaned from the morning meditations, and, over and again, he assured me that this would be the finest retreat of my life.

Frankly, the extraordinarily warm accolades of the dean came as a bit of surprise to me, for I knew something of his life before he was assigned to the Rota in the late 1950s. He had been the priest-secretary of August Cardinal Hlond, the archbishop of Warsaw, who was said to have inappropriately fled Poland when the Second World War broke out. Thus, the mantle of ecclesiastical leadership in Poland fell upon the shoulders of Adam Cardinal Sapheia, the archbishop of Kraków, who in ensuing years suffered greatly at the hands, first of the Nazis, and then of the Communists.

It was he, Cardinal Sapheia, who had called Karol Wojtyla to the priesthood, and it was he who had hidden Karol Wojtyla in his residence throughout the young man's years of theological studies, forming him both intellectually and spiritually.

Whatever of all of this, the dean was exhilarated. "You come from Chicago, where there are many Polish people," he reminded me. "It is important that you hear our retreat master. He has a great mind, one of the greatest in the Church."

The old gentleman unlocked his apartment door and turned around. "Be so good as to be here tomorrow morning at eight, rather than eight-thirty," he said. "We do not want to miss a word. This is a giant, I tell you. Unquestionably, a giant."

Such was my second "encounter" with Pope John Paul II. The third came a few years later.

⌒

In August 1978, the saintly Pope Paul VI passed away. After the funeral, I was approached by a young Vatican lawyer who had been assigned the task of overseeing the conclave that was to elect the next Successor of Saint Peter. He told me that, for centuries, the judges of the Rota had "guarded" the conclave, that he had chosen eight for this duty, and that I was to be one of the group.

At the time, I had been serving on the Rota for a little more than six years but was still the youngest of the fourteen judges. I smiled to myself as I imagined how much genuine "guarding" my aging colleagues and I might be able to do. All the same, I was delighted with the assignment and dutifully took my place each day as a "guard" in the Vatican's "Courtyard of the Parrot" throughout the conclave that elected Pope John Paul I.

After the election and coronation of the new Pontiff, I flew home for my annual vacation. On the day I was to return to Rome, the news outlets of the world announced that John Paul I had died and that another conclave was being convoked.

This time it was felt that only four judges of the Rota were needed, with me as one of their number. Accordingly, I found myself "guarding" the immense vestibule of the Sistine Chapel with an Italian confrère who had been the chancellor of the Rota and was a good friend. Together, we watched the cardinals filing into the chapel on the first day of the conclave. Most entered in groups of two and three, smiling and exchanging pleasantries.

The last to enter, all by himself, was the cardinal archbishop of Kraków. He walked slowly, looking neither to the right nor to the left. The Italian Rota judge asked me if I knew who he was. Before I could answer, the lawyer in charge of the conclave who was standing behind us responded for me.

"That's Wojtyla," he whispered. "He is a man of intense prayer, ever in conversation with the Lord."

Few persons in the Church knew the cardinals of the world as did this lawyer. We accepted his judgment without question.

～

Throughout the years that followed, I had the privilege of many face-to-face "encounters" with Pope John Paul II in audiences of various kinds, in numerous meetings especially about canonical matters, at midday meals, and more. Once, when I was invited to an evening meal, I came unaware that we would be celebrating the Holy Father's name day (November 4, the feast of Saint Charles Borromeo). To the delight of the other guests, the Pope feigned to reprove me for not bringing him a gift or even a card of good wishes.

When I tried to offer an explanation, he laughed and presented me with a gift wrapped in white parchment-like paper and topped with a gold-colored ribbon. It was a portable, battery-powered radio that for many years kept me company in my *belle voiture*. It was also a gesture of kindness for which I shall always be most grateful.

No "encounter" with Pope John Paul II, however, made a deeper impression on me than the one that occurred just two years ago. The occasion was an audience for the students, faculty, and friends of the Pontifical North American College, the seminary in Vatican City that prepares future priests for service in dioceses and archdioceses of the nation.

We were assembled in the Sala Clementina of the Apostolic Palace. A door in the front on the right opened, and the Pope John Paul II entered. He was bent and shuffling. His left hand shook continually, and it was evident that every step he took entailed considerable discomfort.

In view of his physical condition, I expected the Pontiff to go directly to his throne so as to deliver a brief address in response to the customary greetings from the chairman of the board of the college. But the Holy Father had other plans. He went to the center of the front row of the huge crowd before him, turned, and walked toward the right-hand aisle, blessing those on the right side of the front row. He then turned again and walked the length of the right-hand aisle all the way to the rear of the mammoth hall, still blessing the faithful as best he could.

Practice for Heaven

As he returned, walking the length of the left-hand aisle, while still blessing the faithful and struggling with each step, I prayed that he would put an end to what was clearly a "Via Dolorosa" and go immediately to deliver his address.

This, however, was not to be. Instead, he did for the left side of the front row what he had done for the right side, and only then climbed the steps of his throne and, exhausted, sank into it to read a warm welcome and a beautiful reflection on the priesthood from a text presented to him by an evidently concerned priest-secretary.

Three years before, it had been my duty to offer the greetings of the chairman of the board of the college on the occasion of a similar audience, and well do I recall how attentively I listened to the Holy Father's every word. This time, however, I heard very little, for my mind was totally occupied by the image of an aging shepherd of souls utterly careless of his own suffering and lovingly attending to his flock.

When the papal address was concluded, the crowd surged forward and pleaded for photographs. Pope John Paul II limped down the steps from the throne, posed for group photographs, and—to my horror—proceeded laboriously from one side of the front of the hall to the other and back, clasping hands and bestowing blessings. When at last he reached the door through which he had entered and next to which I happened to be standing, he grabbed my arm to steady himself, waved again to the people, and left to go to what I later learned was another audience in an even larger hall.

Hearing the story of the courageous archbishop of Kraków and the church in Nowa Huta; listening to the brilliant retreat master in the chapel in the Papal Palace; watching the cardinal who entered a conclave alone and rapt in prayer; working with him; dining and even celebrating with him — all of these "encounters" and others, too, come together to form my personal and loving portrait of our Holy Father.

None, however, do I treasure more than when I watched in wonder an aging and physically failing shepherd who, like his Lord, was willing to sacrifice himself to the limit so as to welcome, bless, and embrace the flock committed to his care. In my portrait of Pope John Paul II, this will ever be the component that I count the most revealing and most inspiring of all.

Bridgeport, June 1998

Respecting Life

"Read the section of the article that I have marked and never forget it," my friend directed me. "If you are ever hesitant or embarrassed to stand up against that attack on the basics of civilization that is abortion, these few sentences will come in handy. Arthur Rubinstein's mother had 'chosen' to kill him. His aunt 'chose' to take a stand against the killing, and the world was rewarded with one of our greatest musical geniuses."

Starmaker

Eugene Field Playground evokes some of the happiest memories of my childhood. Situated in a village west of Chicago, it boasted a softball field, a swimming pool, and a grassy hill on which we children could run and slide. The centerpiece of the playground, however, was a Tudor-style clubhouse in which we put on our ice skates in the winter and spent many a rainy day in the summer.

The director of the clubhouse was a gentleman by the name of Mr. Polk. He was short, white haired, and always dressed in a suit coat. All of us youngsters were convinced that, if he were not the smartest man on earth, he was certainly among the top ten. He could roundly defeat any challenger in chess or checkers. He could weave an incredibly intricate lariat out of strips of colored leather in a matter of minutes. He could fashion a pair of "real" Indian moccasins that the fiercest brave would be proud to wear.

But, most marvelous of all, Mr. Polk could read *Treasure Island*, *Robinson Crusoe*, *Johnny Tremain*, and the like to a room full of children with such drama that even the most restless would not move a muscle.

My favorite recollection of Mr. Polk, however, was not in the realm of prose, but rather in that of poetry. Our playground was named for the late-nineteenth-century American poet Eugene

Field. In the large meeting room on the main floor of the club-house, all the walls were decorated with splendidly painted murals from waist-high to ceiling, each illustrating one of Field's poems. Even now I can summon quite clearly in my mind's eye the artist's depictions of Wynken, Blynken and Nod, the Gingham Dog and the Calico Cat, Little Boy Blue, and a host of others.

It was in connection with these murals that Mr. Polk had devised one of his most original rainy-day games. He would pass out a printed text of one of Field's poems and give us all ten minutes to commit to memory however much we could. He would then invite all who were so inclined to stand before the mural that corresponded to the poem, hold the printed text behind their backs, and recite as many lines as they were able to remember.

Out of forty or so in the room, maybe eight or nine would rise to the challenge. Still, all participated in the game by sedulously following the text of the poems so as to interrupt when there was a mistake or a lengthy hesitation, and to cheer when a recitation was perfect.

One summer day, as rain pelted the roof of the clubhouse, the poetry game was organized. A little blond girl from the grammar school I attended won easily, not missing a word of the first two verses of Field's "Dutch Lullaby." We all knew what her reward would be. It was always the same, no matter what the game. Mr. Polk would lift a large atlas from the bookshelf behind his desk and draw from it a page of gold-colored foil containing a variety of perforated stars, one of which he would extract from the foil with a casual flick of the hand. The reverse side of the star would then be moistened, and Mr. Polk would press the prize onto the shirt or blouse of the victor.

This particular day, however, the familiar ritual was somewhat altered. Over a period of weeks, a new boy had been coming to the playground. His name was Frankie. He had red hair and freckles, and he also had a heavy cross to bear. For, as we soon learned, he could not express himself except with moans and grimaces, and he could manage even such basic tasks as opening doors only with total concentration and after frequent failed attempts. Thus, he kept very much to himself, watching our games intently, but never joining in.

When the time came to award the star to my little blond schoolmate, Mr. Polk beckoned Frankie to his side. He pulled the atlas from the bookshelf, extracted the page of gold foil, placed it on the desk in front of Frankie, and asked him to tear out the star just as he had seen the clubhouse director do on numerous occasions.

Frankie struggled mightily with the assignment, his tongue clutched between his teeth, and his face growing ever more flushed. We children held our breath, hoping against hope that the endeavor would be crowned with success. At length, with a cry of delight, Frankie raised his arm into the air triumphantly. The star, badly tattered but still recognizable, clung precariously to the tip of his index finger.

Mr. Polk dampened the back of it and returned it to Frankie, who, with a lunge, pressed it onto the blouse of the little blond girl.

"We've been needing a Starmaker around here for a long time," Mr. Polk announced solemnly, "and I believe that we have finally found one. From now on Frankie will be our official Starmaker. I trust that he will always fulfill his duties with fairness, loyalty, and dedication."

The clubhouse was awash with cheers and applause. At first, Frankie only stared at Mr. Polk, tears streaming down his cheeks.

Thereupon, he quite unceremoniously sat down on the floor and emitted such groans of happiness as no poet, even Eugene Field, could ever hope adequately to describe. He had been accepted. He belonged. Even more, he was our Starmaker.

⁓

Toward the end of this past October, I was invited by the Office for Special Education of the Diocese of Bridgeport to a dinner at the Trumbull Marriott Hotel. I was told that perhaps fifty or sixty would be in attendance, and that the purpose of the dinner was to honor the memory of Sister Margaret Mary DiGiacomo, O.P., who until her death last year had been the director of the Special Education Office.

I arrived at the hotel and found well over two hundred guests. Some were special children. Some were special adults. Some were relatives and friends of special people of every age. But all were there to proclaim publicly their gratitude for the sixteen years during which Sister Margaret Mary had served the special community with her own special love and devotion. All had incredibly beautiful stories to tell about the kindness of Sister, perhaps the most touching coming from a boy with Down syn-drome who was afraid not everyone appreciated how deeply he loved "our special Sister."

When the time came for the newly appointed director of the Office for Special Education to present a plaque honoring Sister Margaret Mary to a representative of the Dominican Sisters of Newburgh, I leaned back in my chair and wondered how the honoree might be handling all of this in Heaven.

I dared to hope that in that "special" sector of the Lord's eternal kingdom, where I was certain she would have chosen to reside, Sister had met Frankie. I even dared to guess that, as the plaque was being conferred down here, Frankie was planting a gold foil star on Sister's habit up there. If so, I have no doubt that he did it with style and that she responded with delight.

For she was a star, and she would understand—and cherish—a Starmaker.

Bridgeport, December 1992

Losing Our Grip

The look in his eyes was almost threatening. "Are you a Roman or an Anglican?" he asked, staring at my clerical collar. I tried to ignore him but could not, for his face was inches from mine. "Read chapter 6 of this book," he commanded. "This is how bad things have gotten. We are losing our grip on sanity."

With that he thrust a book into my hands, turned on his heel, and moved toward a nearby staircase. We were on the second floor of a bookstore on the Upper West Side of Manhattan, a bookstore in which the customers are encouraged to browse and are even provided with comfortable chairs in which to sit as they decide on their purchases.

"Read it," my interlocutor called to me as he descended the staircase while peering through wooden columns that supported the handrail. "We are losing our grip—and losing it fast."

⁓

I put the book on the round table from which it had been taken. It was a paperback. On the cover I noticed a photograph of a bearded man and in the title the word *ethics*.

Two other customers had witnessed the scene. One kept her eyes riveted on the volume she was inspecting. The other approached me with a calming smile. "That gentleman comes here often," he reported. "I have always thought him to be quite normal. Perhaps he was just having a bad day."

As I rode home on the train to Bridgeport, and even as I was preparing for Mass the next morning, the angry bookstore customer kept coming to mind. He did seem "quite normal." I was curious to know what had upset him so.

Thus, as soon as I arrived at my office in the Catholic Center a few hours after Mass, I telephoned the bookstore and ordered "the paperback on the round table near the staircase on the second floor with a photograph of a bearded man on the cover and the word *ethics*, in its title." It arrived in three days, and I immediately set myself to reading chapter 6.

≈

The chapter was entitled "Taking Life," and had to do with abortion. It was written in an engaging style, and the first fourteen pages impressed me quite favorably. The author began by asserting that the argument against legalized abortion is "difficult to shake," inasmuch as no one has even been able "to point to any stage in the gradual process [from fertilization to birth] that marks a morally significant dividing line [between the fetus and the child]."

He then addressed himself to attempts at identifying such a "dividing line."

Birth is unacceptable, he maintained, simply because "the fetus/baby is the same entity whether inside or outside the womb.... The location of a being [has nothing to do with] the wrongness of killing it."

Viability, too, is unacceptable, he went on. Just because "the fetus is totally dependent on the mother for its survival," it does not follow it "has no right to life independent of her wishes."

Indeed, "an elderly woman may be totally dependent on her son's looking after her." Still, such dependency hardly confers "the right to kill."

Quickening is likewise unacceptable, he continued. Alleging that "the time when the mother first feels the fetus" might be the point before which it could legitimately be killed is "an outmoded piece of superstition," he opined. For "fetuses do in fact start moving as early as six weeks after fertilization, long before they can be felt to move." Moreover, he added, "the capacity for physical action—or the lack of it—has nothing to do with the seriousness of one's claim on continued life. We do not see, for example, the lack of such capacity as negating the claims of paralyzed people to go on living."

Consciousness is no less unacceptable, he contended, since we do not know when "brain activity," the "capacity to feel pain," and such begin. Hence, he insisted, appealing to an "absence of consciousness" is, at best, a "risky strategy."

Accordingly, the author concluded, "the search for a morally relevant dividing line between the fetus and the newborn baby has failed to yield any event or stage of development that can bear the weight of separating those with a right to life from those who lack such a right."

∽

I was thoroughly pleased with the conclusion and even more pleased with a host of other compelling insights in the next few pages. My pleasure, however, was short-lived. For, after the first fourteen pages, the author's analysis took an unexpected turn. There is no serious argument that can be brought forward to justify abortion, he freely conceded. All the same, he went on, abortion is needed, and the way to render it morally tolerable is to deny the right to live not only to fetuses but also to infants until such a time as they fulfill certain basic expectations.

"The life of a fetus is of no greater value than the life of a non-human animal at a similar level of rationality, self-consciousness, awareness, capacity to feel, etc.," I read to my amazement. "A week-old baby is not a rational and self-conscious being. There are many non-human animals whose rationality, self-consciousness, awareness, capacity to feel, etc. exceed that of a human baby a week or month old. If the fetus does not have the same claim on life as a person, it appears that the newborn baby does not either, and the life of the newborn baby is of less value to it than the life of a pig, a dog, a chimpanzee is to the non-human animal."

The madness flowed on. At one point, the author even suggested that the killing of children up to the age of two or three should not be rejected out of hand. A few confused paragraphs later, though, he felt that it might be more fitting if we simply acted as though "a full legal right to life comes into force ... a short time after birth — perhaps a month."

I set the book down and took a deep breath. It is entitled *Practical Ethics*, was authored by Peter Singer, a professor of Bioethics at Princeton University, was published by the Cambridge University Press in 1993, and on its cover is warmly recommended by the *New York Review of Books* and the *New York Times Higher Education Supplement.*

All of a sudden, I could see in my mind's eye the face of the customer in the bookstore, peering through the railing of the staircase as he was descending. He was 100 percent on target, I told myself. We are indeed losing our grip on sanity — and losing it fast.

How fast?

Losing Our Grip

⁊

A few weeks ago, the president of the United States vetoed a bill passed in both houses of Congress to halt the killing of "beings" of the human species who are outside of their mothers except for the top of their heads. The "beings" are described as "fetuses," and the decision was reported on the evening television news as through it were of interest only to "extremists," "religious fanatics," and the like.

Indeed, senators who frequently lament the plight of hungry children in the "Third World" and members of Congress who are often exercised by the untimely passing of owls and seals, hastened to support the president in their various press conferences. One even characterized the veto as "an act of compassion."

One day, I hope to meet my friend in the bookstore. If I do, I will warmly shake his hand and thank him for being splendidly sane in a society that is clearly losing its grip on sanity and common decency as well — and losing it fast.

Bridgeport, July 1996

Piano Lesson

"She's an old family friend, and she has not been well of late," my caller from the Midwest explained. "Since you live so close to New York, maybe you could look in on her for me. I am afraid she is feeling very much alone."

I did as asked, one week later.

The lady in question was eighty years of age with a mind as sharp as a razor and a wit to match. She welcomed me warmly, invited me to be seated, and promptly disappeared into the kitchen to prepare some tea.

Her apartment was large and elegantly furnished in the style of the 1920s. She had lived in it with her husband, a lawyer, for forty years, and alone for another twenty.

As we drank our tea, my hostess recounted her life story. When she was young, she had dreamed of becoming a concert pianist. Accordingly, her husband, who was always devoted, bought her the magnificent grand piano that graced their living room, and engaged for her the best music teachers available.

"He also bought me something the likes of which you have probably never seen," she announced. "It's that silent spinet in the corner."

"Silent spinet!" I exclaimed. "What in the world is that?"

"They don't make them anymore," she replied with a broad smile. "However, for years I practiced my scales and arpeggios on this one, day after day. It has a little wheel on the side. When it is turned, the keys become harder to press down. It was intended to strengthen my fingers so that I could play as fast as Horowitz."

I went over to the tiny wooden shell of a piano to try it out. With each turn of the wheel on the side, the keys grew more stiff. She was right: I had never seen anything like it.

"And that," she said, pointing to a volume of music on top of the instrument, "is an example of what I used to play many years ago."

It was a collection of Mozart sonatas that had been published in Germany. On the cover the word *Urtext* was printed in large, ornate Gothic letters.

"What does *Urtext* mean?" I inquired.

"It means," she answered with a tinge of sarcasm in her voice, "that these are the original, authentic works of Wolfgang Amadeus Mozart just as he composed them without any addings, subtractings, or editings by folks far less gifted than he."

She rose and approached the silent spinet. "My husband gave me that collection as a birthday gift long, long ago," she reminisced. "You're a pianist. Please take it home with you as a souvenir of our visit. Mozart is well beyond the capacities of these tired old hands of mine."

⬎

Less than two weeks had passed when I received a telephone call from my new friend's physician. She was in the hospital and not doing well. He felt that she would like to see me.

I arrived in the evening during visiting hours. The patient looked very small in her hospital bed.

"It's cancer," she declared with little emotion. "They have started chemotherapy, but there isn't a whole lot of hope. My age is against me."

We chatted, we prayed together, and I gave her my blessing.

A few days later, I telephoned the hospital room and learned that she had returned to her apartment. Thus, on a very warm September morning, I went once again to see her in her home.

This time the door was answered by a visiting nurse. She led me into the living room where my friend was seated in a wheelchair.

"I am glad you came," she said in a low voice. "There is a lot of pain, and I am afraid that there is going to be a lot more."

I tried to allay her fears, but she would have none of it.

"The doctor has been very open with me," she observed. "He said he would be careful to 'alleviate any discomfort,' but I know that there is a limit to what he can do."

"Pain control is an art these days," I insisted. "Let's not be so pessimistic. You are going to beat this. With a lot of good care and a lot of prayers, you are going to be fine, just fine."

The occupant in the wheelchair was not giving my protestations her undivided attention. Rather, as I spoke, she awkwardly rummaged through a pile of papers on a little table at her elbow, quite annoyed that she could not find what she was seeking.

"Last week, I read an article in the *U.S. News and World Report* about a doctor in Michigan who wants to help kill old and sick people who are in a lot of pain," she recounted. "I cut it out but can't seem to find it. Did you see the article?"

I confessed that I had not and nervously endeavored to change the subject.

"You shouldn't be reading that kind of thing," I said. "You should be focusing on getting well. And you ought to have a television set."

"Would television help me focus on getting well?" she retorted playfully. "I'm a reader, and I have always been a reader. I like to keep up on things by reading about them."

Suddenly, for no reason evident to me, the playfulness drained from her face. She reached out to take my hand and signaled me to draw my chair closer to hers.

"The Lord gave me my life," she announced, "but it is still His, not mine. I have it only on loan. If He wants me, I will go gladly. If He decides that I should stay, I will stay and make the best of it. That, dear Bishop, has always been my Catholic belief, and I know no reason to abandon it now. Indeed, over the past several months, as difficult as they have been, I have learned to hold on to it even tighter."

As she spoke, my eyes settled on the silent spinet in the corner behind her, the curious little wooden mechanism that had made her fingers stronger when they were forced to press harder; and somehow I knew that, whatever the future might bring, she would handle it with courage and, above all, faith.

⌒

The funeral was in December, in Saint Ignatius Loyola Church on Park Avenue. It was a snowy day, and there were few in church. Accordingly, my homily was quite brief. Indeed, virtually all that I did in the pulpit was recite and reflect on the words of Saint Paul in the fourteenth chapter of his letter to the Romans: "None of us lives to himself, and none of us dies to himself. If we live, we live to the Lord, and if we die, we die to the Lord; so then, whether we live or whether we die, we are the Lord's" (Rom. 14:7–8).

This was my text. Or, better, my *Urtext*. For I was keenly aware that the deceased had both understood and embraced the teaching of the Apostle and would have little patience with "addings, subtractings, or editings."[15]

Bridgeport, April 1994

---

[15] In her will, Cardinal Egan's friend bequeathed her treasured Steinway grand piano to the Diocese of Bridgeport, where it was placed in Saint Augustine Cathedral.

A Decent People

It is March of 1857. Two men are seated at a table in an inn on the outskirts of a small town in southwestern Connecticut. One has just read a newspaper account of a decision by the Supreme Court in Washington, D.C.[16]

This might have been the conversation that ensued.

⁓

"Look at this, Reuben. The Supreme Court has finally concluded the litigation about the slave Dred Scott."

"What did they decide, Simon?"

"Scott was a slave and didn't stop being a slave just because his master had taken him to live for a while in Illinois, where slavery is outlawed. That's what they decided."

"So he can be bought and sold, beaten and killed by his owner just the same as always?"

---

[16] On March 6, 1857, the U.S. Supreme Court decided in *Dred Scott v. Sanford* that African-Americans, whether enslaved or free, could not be U.S. citizens and therefore had no rights under U.S. law. The ruling was overturned after the Civil War by the Civil Rights Act of 1866 and the Fourteenth Amendment to the U.S. Constitution in 1868.

"That's correct, Reuben. The Supreme Court has spoken. The matter's finally been put to rest forever."

"Does it bother you, Simon, that slaves at least appear to be human beings, you know, persons with a God-given right not to be killed by private parties?"

"Well, sort of. But I always say that owners must have the right to choose."

"The right to choose what?"

"You're not supposed to ask that, Reuben. When fashionable folk say 'the right to choose,' they never say what they're choosing. That would ruin everything."

"But, Simon, don't slaves have eyes and ears like you and me? Can't slaves think and talk? No one had ever proved that they're not human beings with 'an unalienable right to live,' as our own Declaration of Independence puts it. I'm not wrong about this, am I?"

"No, but you're pushing the thing too far. Just say 'right to choose' quickly without thinking what is being chosen, and you won't feel so bad. And if you still have a conscience problem, try saying 'right to privacy.'"

"What in the world does that have to do with anything?"

"Well, Reuben, look at it this way. When a slave owner is killing his slave, he doesn't want the government to be snooping around the plantation and interfering because his privacy is sacred. 'Right to privacy' is the tailor-made slogan for people who are uncomfortable about the killing of slaves. All the clever people use it when troublesome types ask, for example, what is being chosen by those who have 'a right to choose.' It saves folks from a heap of embarrassment."

"Simon, I am beginning to think you are either the most dishonest or the most foolish man I've ever met. Suppose you were visiting me one night in my home, we got into an argument, and I got my shotgun to kill you. Should the government not get involved because I have 'a right to privacy'?"

"Of course not, Reuben. But you're missing the point. 'Right to privacy' is like 'right to choose.' It's something to say when someone confronts you about the issue of slaves and their being killed by their owners. And it's nothing more than that."

"I can't believe what I'm hearing, Simon. What has gotten into you?"

⁓

"Very well, Reuben, if you don't like 'right to choose' and 'right to privacy,' there is something else that always works in these kinds of awkward conversations."

"Tell me. I am all ears."

"Fine. As you know, Reuben, Quakers are against slavery, against the buying and selling of slaves, against beating them, and against killing them too. So, if you want to put an end to an unpleasant discussion about slaves and their rights, you just say that Quakers and other religious fanatics who oppose the killing of slaves are trying to force their religious 'dogmas' on the rest of us. And, for good measure, add that they are also 'breaking down the wall between church and state.'"

"I don't like to have to say this, Simon, but that's nonsense, and you know it. No one but a helpless bigot would buy into that kind of rubbish."

"A bigot!"

"Yes, a bigot. Whether the Quakers or any other religious folk are for or against the right of slave owners to kill their slaves is completely beside the point. The one and only question is whether our government, or any civilized government for that matter, is free to stand aside when a private party is killing a being that gives every indication of being a human being, and no indication of being anything but a human being. A human being, Simon, just like you and me."

"Well, if you put it that way ..."

⁀

"Listen, Simon, no more meaningless formulas to cover up the obvious, no more attempts to escape the most fundamental demands of justice by making religious folks scapegoats. Let's cut to the chase. Let me ask you a question. Your wife is pregnant, isn't she?"

"Yes, she is, Reuben."

"Now, that being inside of her is growing eyes and ears and all the rest just like you and me, isn't it?"

"Yes, certainly."

"Well, Simon, if we keep accepting the killing of slaves on the basis of silly nonsense, it might one day occur to sophisticated folks that there's no reason why private parties can't rightly kill the creatures inside their mothers, too. Of course, no one would ever be able to prove that creatures inside their mothers are anything but human beings with rights, including the right to live. Still, it is no less true that no one could ever prove that slaves are anything but human beings with rights, including the right to live.

"If we can push all logic and common sense into the background with ridiculous slogans and such when there is question of the killing of slaves," Reuben continued, "we can do the same when there is question of ... I hate to say the word, but I'm going to anyway—when there is question of abortion."

A Decent People

"Are you suggesting, Reuben, that the government of the United States would ever look the other way when private parties choose to kill creatures within their mothers the way it allows slave owners to kill their slaves? Are you daring to imagine that such an outrage could even be considered in this noble land of ours? You should be ashamed of yourself. We are far too decent people for anything like that."

"Simon, my friend," Reuben said, "I pray to God that we are."

Bridgeport, October 1992

Costco and Mayonnaise

On Sunday, July 18, I was in Tacoma, Washington, to address and celebrate Mass for the Catholic Daughters of the Americas at their biennial convention. Hence, I did not see the Sunday New York newspapers until several days later. A pile of them were stacked up in the office of the archbishop's residence. I did not get to them until the following Thursday night at around eleven o'clock.

In the magazine section of one of the newspapers, I noticed an article entitled "When One Is Enough." At first, I took it for a rather tasteless parody of the pro-abortion mentality. However, the newspaper in which it was printed is a fierce champion of abortion. Thus, I realized it could not be what it seemed at first blush. Accordingly, I read the article carefully, and I was sickened.

The author of the piece was "Amy Richards as told to Amy Barrett." Amy Richards is presented as a thirty-four-year-old woman, living with her "boyfriend" in a "five-story walk-up" in the East Village, and working as a "freelance" writer. She reports that she had stopped using "the Pill" because she was "tired of it"; and she adds that her boyfriend approved. They would let whatever happened, happen.

In due course, Amy Richards became pregnant with triplets. She was totally unnerved, and she explains why. Apart from the usual inconveniences of pregnancy and motherhood, the triplets would guarantee her an altogether unacceptable future.

"I'm going to have to move to Staten Island," she declares. "I'll never leave my house because I'll have to take care of these children. I'll have to start shopping only at Costco and buying big bottles of mayonnaise." Such was her plight, as described by the writer, Amy Barrett, for the freelance writer Amy Richards.

What was Amy Richards to do? She made her decision, and if I understand the tortuous prose of the article, her boyfriend agreed. She would have two of the triplets killed by a "specialist" known to her obstetrician. How the specialist would handle this is described twice in the 800-word article: "The procedure involves a shot of potassium chloride in the heart of the fetus." And when the "procedure" is completed, Amy Richards confides, "two [of the triplets] disappear."

The incredibly ugly article ends thus: "I would do the same thing if I had triplets again, but if I had twins, I would probably have the twins. Then again, I don't know."

⁓

A few days later, in another New York newspaper we are informed that the Amy Richards of "When One Is Enough" is not at all the coarse, fatuous individual she is made out to be in the article, but rather a college-educated "consultant" to one of the most prosperous and "upscale" providers of abortion in the national abortion industry. A spokesperson for the newspaper that hosted the article was allegedly considering "an editor's note" to clear up any suggestion that the article may have been intentionally misleading.

Whatever of this, the article, as crass and abhorrent as it might be, may have some peripheral value. It could lead decent, thoughtful people who have been frightened into silence by the pro-abortion media of communications to speak out on the subject. If so, here are some observations that may be of interest.

First, if the being that was within the mother's womb is an innocent human being with an inalienable right to live one minute after it has left its mother's womb, how can anyone be sure that it was not an innocent human being with an inalienable right to live one minute before it left its mother's womb, or one month before, or nine months before?

To pretend not to understand the implications of this query is a choice, and to act on that pretense is another choice — a choice to kill what cannot be shown to be other than an innocent human being with an inalienable right to live.

Second, one may not in any civilized society kill what has never been shown to be other than an innocent human being with an inalienable right to live; and this is true quite apart from any consideration of this religion or that or, indeed, of any religion at all. A healthy religion might be expected to second and applaud such a basic principle of civilization, just as a healthy religion might be expected to second and applaud the unacceptability in civilized society of armed robbery. However, seconding and applauding does not make armed robbery "a solely religious issue," any more than it makes abortion "a solely religious issue."

To pretend not to understand this is a choice; and when the choice is made in order to cover the failure of legislators and judges to deal with the matter of abortion honorably, it is an unacceptable choice indeed. Worse yet, it is a betrayal of civilized society and the most fundamental right of mankind, the right to live.

Third, even if legislatures and courts, along with kings and presidents, contend that we are free to kill what has never been shown to be other than an innocent human being with an inalienable right to live, this changes nothing for the rest of us. We, as members of civilized society, are obliged to stand for what is clear, basic, and true in this world in which we live.

Have we forgotten how bitterly we condemned the military officers who claimed that they properly killed millions of citizens of Georgia in the former Soviet Union because Stalin, the leader of their government, favored the killing? Have we forgotten how bitterly we condemned the medical practitioners who claimed they properly killed millions of Jews in Germany because Hitler, the leader of their government, favored the killing?

If we have forgotten, why?

∾

When I was a boy many years ago, I studied music with great enthusiasm and even dreamed of becoming a concert pianist. Among my heroes was the Polish keyboard master Arthur Rubinstein. I believed then, as I believe now, that no one in our time performed the works of Frédéric Chopin with the artistry that flowed from his fingers.

Some time ago, a friend of mine sent me an old copy of *Time* magazine (February 25, 1966), asking me to give special attention to the cover story about Rubinstein, and especially to the paragraph that he underscored. The paragraph read as follows:

> Rubinstein was born in 1887, in the shabby industrial town of Lodz, in Poland, where his father owned a small

hand-loom factory. He was the last of seven children. "My mother did not want a seventh child," he explains, "so she decided to get rid of me before I was born. Then, a marvelous thing happened. My aunt dissuaded her, and so I was permitted to be born."

My friend reminded me that I had told him that I admired Rubinstein immensely, that I had purchased all of his recordings that I could afford when I was young, and that I had virtually worn the wax off my 78 rpm records of his performance of the Chopin sonatas.

"Read the section of the article that I have marked and never forget it," my friend directed me. "If you are ever hesitant or embarrassed to stand up against that attack on the basics of civilization that is abortion, these few sentences will come in handy. Rubinstein's mother had 'chosen' to kill him. His aunt 'chose' to take a stand against the killing, and the world was rewarded with one of our greatest musical geniuses.

"The promoters of abortion are going to try to convince the man on the street, and the woman, too, that abortion is purely a matter of one's religious faith," he continued, "and some who have political obligations in this area are going to suggest that, while they are 'personally' opposed to abortion for religious reasons, they will not force their religious beliefs on others. All of this is manifest nonsense which by no means trumps the crystal-clear truth that, long before religion enters into the fray, abortion is, and always was, a patent violation of an altogether fundamental rule of civilized life.

"This is truth," he concluded, "and we have to trust that one day truth will triumph here in this beloved nation of yours and mine."

Practice for Heaven

I put the letter down (it had been paper-clipped to the issue of *Time*) and took from my collection of recordings Rubinstein's rendition of B minor and B-flat minor sonatas of Chopin. With the magical art of this wondrous artist in the background, I re-read the final quotation of my boyhood hero in the *Time* article. Here it is:

> I'm passionately involved in life: I love its change, its color, its movement. To be alive, to be able to speak, to see, to walk, to have houses, music, paintings — it's all a miracle.

"Yes," I mused to myself, "life *is* a miracle. However, before we get into miracles and other matters of a religious kind, we do well to recall that, miraculous or not, to live is first and foremost a right, a right that none of us is free to leave undefended."

New York, September 2004

Someone Who Doesn't Love Them?

The Children's Rehabilitation Center is one of the proudest boasts of Catholic health care in the Archdiocese of New York. It is located in White Plains and cares for youngsters with the most serious of physical and psychological disabilities. In the fall, I had the pleasure of visiting the Center in the company of its gifted and dedicated medical director, Dr. Maria Pici, and members of its staff and its board of directors.

We moved from room to room. In one, tots with Down syndrome, spinal bifida, and the disabling effects of meningitis were being led through games designed to teach them to identify shapes and colors. In another, older children who could not see or speak were being cleverly instructed by means of rhythm and music. And in all, highly professional doctors, nurses, and staff persons were showering upon their young charges the best that medical science has to offer, plus a measure of love and compassion that could not help but touch the heart.

One room, however, made a particularly deep impression on me. On its floor was spread a gymnast's mat on which lay a young doctor. In front of him was a kind of highchair in which sat a boy of four years. The boy, José by name, was picking up little Styrofoam balls with the toes of his left foot and carefully placing them in a brightly colored basket situated on the mat between him and the doctor. With each success, the doctor applauded enthusiastically, and José smiled broadly.

Why was this child using the toes of his left foot to pick up the Styrofoam balls? Because he had no right foot, and no hands or arms either. He was just the trunk of a boy, one leg, a head covered with shiny black hair, and a face with a smile that lit up the room.

Before long, I found myself applauding along with the doctor, and with each burst of applause José rewarded me with one of his glorious smiles.

<hr />

That evening, I was back in my residence on Madison Avenue. On the floor next to my desk stood a pile of publications of various kinds that I had saved over a period of weeks to read whenever there was a free moment. The two on top were newsmagazines. On the covers of both were sonogram photographs of babies within their pregnant mothers. The photographs on the covers and inside the magazines as well were nothing short of astounding. One could see everything with crystalline clarity. The beings within their mothers had round little bodies, two arms, two legs, heads on which some had hair, hands which some were waving, and faces on which were found, in several of the photographs, bright, beautiful smiles.

The theme of both of the articles illustrated by the sonogram photographs was, in effect, a question: Would it be right to kill these little beings?

The articles were written with careful attention to political correctness. Thus, for the most part, they avoided asking if it would be legitimate to kill the beings in the photographs, preferring to speculate as to whether it would be legitimate to choose to kill them, somehow suggesting that choosing to kill is perhaps less blameworthy than simply killing.

Similarly, both articles were careful to avoid, where they could, the use of the words *babies* and *children* to identify the beings under discussion with their little bodies, two arms, two legs, waving hands, and smiles. Hence, the beings were regularly styled "fetuses," again perhaps to suggest that it might be less offensive to kill or choose to kill them if they bore an unfamiliar and antiseptic designation.

As I studied the photographs, I could not get José out of my mind. Might we properly kill or choose to kill him, I asked myself, at least if we were to invent some medical-sounding Latin expression like *puerulus*, for example, to take the place of "little boy" in discussing him?

Would it thus be ethical, moral, honorable, decent, or — if you will — other than manifestly evil to "terminate his life" or choose to "terminate his life," given his at least appearing to be somewhat less than what one might expect of an ideal human being endowed by the Creator with an inalienable right to live?

⁓

For anyone who ever had the pleasure of being with José and his doctor in the Children's Rehabilitation Center, I have no doubt that the answer would be loudly and clearly in the negative.

True, José does not have the arms that most human beings have and that the "fetuses" in the sonogram photographs clearly have. True, José does not have the two legs that most human beings have and that the "fetuses" in the sonogram photographs clearly have. True, José does not wave his arms as most human beings do and as several of the "fetuses" do as well. Whatever of this, he does smile as most human beings do and as several of the "fetuses" in the sonogram photographs also do; and, if we are to believe some of our greatest philosophers, there could be no more telling and compelling proof of his humanity.

Accordingly, even if someone should wish to call him *puerulus* or anything else for that matter, killing him, no more or less than choosing to kill him, would be an outrage.

And, if all of this is true, what about the beings within their mothers, the beings in the sonogram photographs? Are they ethically able to be killed or chosen for killing? Would "terminating their lives" be any less wicked than doing the same for José?

Some would seem to answer that the beings within their mothers are fair game to be killed or chosen for killing, but the same cannot be said of José. Their reasons, although never more than hinted at, appear to be as follows.

~

First, the beings in the sonogram photographs are within their mothers; and for this reason their lives can be licitly snuffed out. Were they elsewhere, the situation would be different. For me, this point of view has always evoked a rather special repugnance, and the reason is quite personal.

When I was a boy, I contracted a form of infantile paralysis known as "bulbar poliomyelitis." Victims of this malady were at that time often placed for life within huge steel cases known as "iron lungs," outside of which they could not breathe or live. I was fortunate enough to have escaped this horror, but knew of and had seen photographs of a young man in a neighboring village who had not escaped it. My parents were friends of the young man's parents, and their admiration of them, and sympathy for them, knew no limit.

From hearing my father and mother speak about the matter, I was quite secure that, whatever happened to me, wherever I had to be put, I would be protected, cared for, and loved. My location within the steel case, or anywhere else, would not make me anything less than Edward Egan, son of Thomas and Genevieve.

Second, some would feel (it could hardly be more than a feeling) that unlike the beings within their mothers, José is not to be deprived of his life because we can see him and thus recognize him to be a human being, a person much like ourselves, although considerably unlike ourselves in several rather important aspects. Why being able to be seen — or even heard, touched, or smelled — would have any relevance as regards one's right to live, I am not sure.

All the same, whatever the thought processes behind this unusual "feeling," events have contrived to render them utterly invalid. For, thanks to the sonogram photographs, we now see the beings within their mothers, the beings with their arms, legs, waving hands, and smiles. Indeed, we see them with marvelous clarity, and we know exactly and precisely what we are seeing.

Was there ever a time when one could with honor maintain that the beings within their mothers might be legitimately killed because there was no secure and certain knowledge as to what they were? We leave that to historians. For, if there ever were such a time, it has surely passed. Look at the photographs on the covers of the two newsmagazines and the other photographs inside as well, and you will see everything clearly, poignantly, and inescapably.

⁓

The Children's Rehabilitation Center is blessed with a splendid swimming pool in which children are exercised by skilled doctors and nurses in swimming suits and goggles. The room in which the pool is located brought back bittersweet memories of a similar facility in which I had been assisted by doctors and nurses to rebuild my arms, legs, and back after polio many years ago.

As we stood next to the pool, listening to the playful cries of the children echoing back and forth against the tile walls and listening, as well, to an explanation of the effectiveness of the pool for children with certain forms of paralysis, something else was tenaciously tugging at my mind and heart.

Thus it was that, with no sufficient preamble, I interrupted the conversation to ask Dr. Pici, "What about José? What is going to become of him?"

Dr. Pici took hold of my arm. "Don't worry about José," she said. "He's a bright little boy. He will make it. Trust me, he will do just fine. Everyone here loves him, and everyone here feels just as you do."

"And the children in the sonogram photographs?" I asked myself that evening as I sat at my desk inspecting the newsmagazines. "Is there someone who doesn't love them?"

New York, February 2004

282

The Pontiff and the Policeman

The Mass was scheduled for the last Friday in September. In attendance were to be laypersons involved in a variety of volunteer programs, such as visiting the sick in hospitals, bringing the Eucharist to nursing-home residents, and tutoring young people in center-city schools.

I was searching for a homily theme a few weeks before the Mass and happened upon an article in a New York newspaper that seemed to offer a promising point of departure.

A young man from East Harlem had died in a motorcycle accident just three days after being released from prison. The reason for the imprisonment was both dramatic and tragic. At the age of fifteen, with no apparent provocation, he had shot a policeman, rendering him for life a quadriplegic who depended on a respirator.

A reporter, according to the newspaper article, had approached the policeman for a comment on the death of the young man. The reply was stunning. The policeman announced that he had forgiven his assailant immediately; that he had frequently sought to be of help to him during his imprisonment; and that he had continually prayed that one day he would "find peace and purpose to his life."

The article explained the policeman's reaction in terms quite unexpected from a publication generally unfriendly to the Church. The policeman thought and acted as he did, it alleged, "because of his Roman Catholic faith."

"What facet of that faith could provoke such a reaction?" I asked in my homily. "The love of God for all humanity; the willingness of Jesus Christ to die for every son and daughter of His heavenly Father; and the injunction of the Gospel that we treat all others as we would be treated," were among my answers.

However, I insisted, the most fundamental reply harkens back to the very origins and nature of our species.

If we truly believe that every human being, no matter how odious he or she may be, is created "in the image and likeness of God," and therefore endowed with a preciousness that knows no boundary, our options in reacting to the misdeeds of others are extraordinarily limited. We may never hate. We may never bear grudges. We may never refuse our care or exclude from our prayer any of those "mirrors held up to the Divinity" which include every person the Almighty ever fashioned.

⁀

The following Saturday found me in Yonkers, at Saint Joseph's Seminary of the Archdiocese of New York, along with forty-two of the seminarians of the Diocese of Bridgeport. We were there to join Pope John Paul II for evening prayer.

The seminary chapel and grounds were filled with candidates for the priesthood from New York, New Jersey, and Connecticut, and thousands of laity and religious from the Yonkers area. At the conclusion of the ceremony, the bishops led the Holy Father and his party out of the chapel.

The Pontiff and the Policeman

Coming down the steps of the seminary, I noticed, on the lawn directly ahead of me, a wheelchair in which sat a former policeman who was breathing with the help of a respirator. I had been with him and his wife a number of times after he was shot by a young man of fifteen. Hence, he greeted me warmly, and she came from behind the wheelchair to take my hand and initiate a conversation.

A roar went up from the clusters of photographers who were stationed on all sides. "Out of the way," they pleaded. "You're blocking our view."

I moved quickly down the road and, looking back, could see in the glare of floodlights and flashbulbs an elderly cleric in a white cassock embracing the man in the wheelchair. I could not hear what they were saying, but I do know that each in his own way has been for years teaching all who will listen the most basic of lessons about humanity, its dignity, and its obligations. [17]

An itinerant Preacher had proclaimed that lesson almost two millennia ago in a land called Galilee. We are to love our enemies and to pray for those who persecute us, He said: and all of this because we have been modeled—each without exception—in the likeness of our "one Father in Heaven."

The policeman from his wheelchair repeats that lesson to newspaper reporters and to all who see him, whether in the streets of New York or even at a seminary in Yonkers.

The Pontiff heralds it from pulpits across the world, and even from a podium of the United Nations.

---

[17] New York Police Department Detective Steven McDonald, paralyzed by an assailant's bullet on July 12, 1986, met Pope John Paul II during the Holy Father's visit to New York City in October 1995.

Practice for Heaven

The Preacher embraces them both and invites us to join in delivering their—and His—message.

It is not at all complicated, He maintains: Love your neighbor as yourself, for you are all children of the one Lord, Who created you in a burst of divine charity and "in His image and likeness."

Bridgeport, November 1995

Men and Women for Others

Our book concludes, not with another column, but with a moving homily delivered by Cardinal Egan in Saint Patrick's Cathedral on September 11, 2002. The occasion was a Memorial Mass for those who died or were injured in the terrorist attack on the World Trade Center on September 11, 2001, and for their relatives and friends. The cardinal often referred to Ground Zero as "Ground Hero."

My dear friends:

A year has passed since the terrorists attacked. We were taken by surprise. We were shocked. We were wounded. We were grievously wounded. Evil had had its moment of triumph in Lower Manhattan.

This is, therefore, an anniversary that stings and sears the soul. It thrusts us back into an experience of such infamy as none of us might ever have imagined. Thousands of good and decent citizens of Greater New York were brutally murdered. An ugly chasm was dug into the heart of our city; and in the hearts of countless mothers and fathers, brothers and sisters, wives and husbands, children and grandchildren, friends and coworkers, there even now aches the nagging pain of loss for persons dearly loved and sorely needed.

Practice for Heaven

All the same, from the crime of September 11, 2001, we have learned a powerful lesson that we must never let slip from our memories. It is simply this: When truly challenged, the best of us forget ourselves and become men and women for others; men and women who march into harm's way for others; men and women who are even willing to give their lives for others.

In a bustling, competitive metropolis like ours, the citizenry can become quite self-absorbed. "If you can make it here, you can make it anywhere," we sing, and "making it" is understood to require focus — focus largely on ourselves.

Thus, in our strivings and struggles, we can seem to be a people insensitive to the needs of others, a people who take little note of the weak, the frightened, and the hurting. This is, in fact, what many thought of us until that dreadful morning when the terrorists came to do us harm.

Then we learned — perhaps even to our own surprise — that within the hearts of the best of us there resides a goodness that is incredibly selfless. We learned that, when summoned by great events, we become in great numbers remarkably committed to the well-being of others, even total strangers. We become a strong people, a courageous people, a noble people — a people for others.

~

A young doctor stands in front of Saint Vincent's Hospital in scrubs. He has witnessed the slow and sickening collapse of the North Tower of the World Trade Center. His father worked in an office on the 102nd floor. He is trembling, but will not leave his post. He stands there with other doctors and nurses surrounded by wheelchairs and gurneys covered with glistening white sheets. He is urged to go into the hospital, to sit down, to have a cup of coffee, to grieve.

"I am a doctor," he whispers. "The injured will be coming shortly. My place is here."

This is not a character out of fiction. This is not an imaginary hero. This is one of us.

On September 11, a police commander has inhaled the infected dust and soot that engulfed the area around the fallen towers. His doctors inform him that his lungs are being damaged. On September 12, he leads his fellow police officers through the horror that has come to be called Ground Zero, careless of his own condition and all but offended by the suggestion that he go home for rest and medical attention.

"I am staying right here," he announces, and stay he does.

This is not a character out of fiction. This is not an imaginary hero. This is one of us.

A team of emergency workers digs into broken cement and pools of oily mud to pull half-dead and dead bodies out from under piles of debris. They stop only to breathe a prayer for a victim being folded into a shiny, plastic body bag, or to send up a shout of joy when a dust-covered form emerges, as from out of a tomb, and shows signs of life. They labor around the clock, day after day, asking nothing but to be allowed to continue. They are exhausted, and they know that, at any moment, their own lives might be snuffed out by a falling steel beam or a dislodged block of granite. Still, they work on — and on and on.

These are not characters out of fiction. These are not imaginary heroes. Each one is one of us.

A firefighter has made it to the 28th floor of the North Tower. Men and women, half-blinded and gripped with fear, follow his deep, confident voice down narrow, slippery stairs. When all are able to fend for themselves, the firefighter turns and climbs back into the inferno above to shepherd others to safety. He is overcome by smoke. He falls lifeless on the stairs, while his helmet bounces with a thud to the landing below.

This is not a character out of fiction. This is not an imaginary hero. This is one of us.

～

Some, like myself, were privileged to be eyewitnesses to these magnificent demonstrations of courage and self-sacrifice. Others learned of them and others like them from newspaper accounts, radio reports, and images on the television.

For several days, even weeks, following September 11, 2001, it was as though our entire community and, indeed, all of the nation were transported into some huge house of worship to be inspired by sermons delivered not in words but, rather, in deeds of incredible heroism and total selflessness.

In this venerable cathedral, for over a century and a half, the words of our Gospel this evening have been read and preached hundreds, no, thousands, of times. The Lord commands us to love one another as He has loved us and adds that there is no greater love than this, that one lay down his life for another. Preacher after preacher has repeated this message — a message of holiness at its zenith. But none have delivered it with the power with which it was delivered by the heroes of September 11, 2001.

The terrorists accomplished their heinous purposes. We cannot deny the immense and long-lasting harm they have done. Nonetheless, their evil begot a lesson in goodness that can never be recalled or meditated enough.

Here in this city, when challenged by the most horrendous of events, men and women just like ourselves exhibited a love of neighbor beyond anything any of us might have expected. They proved how strong and noble we can be and gave us a measure against which to judge ourselves and our way of life throughout the years that lie ahead.

Nor were they alone in all of this. Immediately after the attack, individuals and teams of individuals from New Jersey, Connecticut, Pennsylvania, Washington, the South, the Midwest, the West, and even foreign lands came in great numbers to stand and struggle alongside our heroes, asking nothing but to be of help. We can never thank them enough. They, too, gifted us with a precious lesson in goodness.

Similarly, we can never sufficiently express our gratitude to the president who joined us in our travail; the governor who guided us at every step; the mayor who wisely and mightily led us; and the commissioners of the police department, the fire department, and the emergency services who directed and inspired our heroes.

⁂

Tonight, we join in prayer for all of these and all of their counterparts in our nation's capital and in Pennsylvania as well. Tonight, too, we lift our minds and hearts to our heavenly Father on behalf of those who were lost in the terror of September 11, their families and loved ones, the injured, and all who have suffered in our common tragedy.

We listen to the words of the Hebrew Scriptures read to us just a few minutes ago. The Lord is with the upright, they tell us. If we are just, honorable, and virtuous, we will be ever in His providential care. And our city—the inspired words conclude—"our city will rejoice" (cf. Proverbs 11:10).

⁂

In 2013, in notes compiled for a planned autobiography, Cardinal Egan wrote of "two stories about 9/11 that might further illuminate the human side of the tragedy." They are included here as a reminder of the cardinal's pastoral presence during this tortuous time.

⁀

In front of Saint Vincent's Hospital on September 11, there stood a young doctor who was in scrubs and trembling. I asked what was the matter, and he replied that his father was killed when the second tower was attacked. I invited him to come inside the hospital, where the Sisters had left tea and coffee for me in a little room next to the main door.

"Thank you, Your Eminence," he said, "but this is my place. I am a doctor, and more who have been injured will soon be here."

Some months later, I was in Rome for a finance-committee meeting, after which Pope John Paul II invited me to lunch. In the course of our conversation, I told him about the young doctor. He asked me if he had completed his studies, and I replied that he still needed to do an internship and a residency.

"Find out how much that will cost," the Holy Father said, "and I will send him a gift to assist him."

A few months later, Archbishop Leonardo Sandri, the substitute secretary of state, joined the doctor and me at Ground Zero to present a check from the Holy Father to the doctor, as the three of us stood in front of the celebrated 9/11 Cross that was formed by two pieces of steel rising above the rubble.

⁀

The second story has to do with an incident ten years later. Hundreds of New York City firefighters were assembled in Avery Fisher Hall at Lincoln Center to commemorate the tenth anniversary of 9/11. I was one of the speakers, and as I was about to go up on stage, the new fire commissioner of the City of New York stopped me.

"I have always been wanting to tell you this, Cardinal," he said. "On the day after the 9/11 attack, I was hit by a falling object and lying on the ground semiconscious. You approached me, knelt down, and shouted into my ear that you were absolving me of my sins and anointing me, too. It was dark, so I couldn't see you, but I knew it was you."

"How?" I asked.

"Everyone knows that voice of yours," he replied with a laugh.

Sophia Institute

Sophia Institute is a nonprofit institution that seeks to nurture the spiritual, moral, and cultural life of souls and to spread the Gospel of Christ in conformity with the authentic teachings of the Roman Catholic Church.

Sophia Institute Press fulfills this mission by offering translations, reprints, and new publications that afford readers a rich source of the enduring wisdom of mankind.

Sophia Institute also operates two popular online Catholic resources: CrisisMagazine.com and CatholicExchange.com.

Crisis Magazine provides insightful cultural analysis that arms readers with the arguments necessary for navigating the ideological and theological minefields of the day. *Catholic Exchange* provides world news from a Catholic perspective as well as daily devotionals and articles that will help you to grow in holiness and live a life consistent with the teachings of the Church.

In 2013, Sophia Institute launched Sophia Institute for Teachers to renew and rebuild Catholic culture through service to Catholic education. With the goal of nurturing the spiritual, moral, and cultural life of souls, and an abiding respect for the role and work of teachers, we strive to provide materials and programs that are at once enlightening to the mind and ennobling to the heart; faithful and complete, as well as useful and practical.

Sophia Institute gratefully recognizes the Solidarity Association for preserving and encouraging the growth of our apostolate over the course of many years. Without their generous and timely support, this book would not be in your hands.

www.SophiaInstitute.com
www.CatholicExchange.com
www.CrisisMagazine.com
www.SophiaInstituteforTeachers.org

Sophia Institute Press® is a registered trademark of Sophia Institute.
Sophia Institute is a tax-exempt institution as defined by the
Internal Revenue Code, Section 501(c)(3). Tax I.D. 22-2548708.